What is feminism?

What is feminism?

An introduction to feminist theory

Chris Beasley

Publications
usand Oaks • New Delhi

First published in 1999 by
Allen & Unwin
9 Atchison Street
St Leonards NSW 1590
Australia

 SAGE Publications Ltd
6 Bonhill Street
London EC2A 4PU

SAGE Publications Inc
2455 Teller Road
Thousand Oaks, California 91320

SAGE Publications India Pvt Ltd
32, M-Block Market
Greater Kailash—I
New Delhi 110 048

British Library Cataloguing in Publication data

A catalogue record for this book is available from the
British Library

ISBN 978-0-7619-6334-9 (hbk)
ISBN 978-0-7619-6335-6 (pbk)

Library of Congress catalog record available

10 9 8 7 6 5 4 3 2 1

To my good friend Christine Putland, who suggested the overall form of this volume and offered several valuable suggestions; to Peter Hall, for extraordinary generosity and patience in difficult times, not to mention a number of design contributions; and to our daughter, Perry Grace, for her utter disinterest in my completion of anything unrelated to her small, lively self.

Contents

Introduction

Feminism is a troublesome term. It may conjure up images of lively discussions, gesticulating hands and perhaps the occasional thumping of fists on tables; certainly, hot milk and bedsocks do not spring to mind. And yet, while the term appears to encourage a great many people to express opinions, it is by no means clear what is being talked about.

Such lack of clarity is not a straightforward result of either limited knowledge or prejudiced misrepresentation. Feminism is one of those terms that inconveniently defy simple explanation. Moreover, feminism's complexity and diversity provide obstacles to those wishing to gain a satisfactory grasp of its meanings. This interesting and powerful combination initially suggested to me the need for a short, comprehensive and intellectually rigorous book, a book which could deal with the question of what characterises contemporary Western feminism. I chose the somewhat impatient query, 'What *is* feminism anyway?', as the appropriate title for this book in order to signal my growing perception that although the term 'feminism' is commonly used it is, at the same time, both confusing and difficult.[1]

This book is intended to be used as a helpful, condensed but thorough reference by those of you who are new to the field as well as those who are already well informed. It offers both analysis and a survey—an accessible, short-cut through the swathe of writing dealing with feminism. After reading the book you should be able to launch into a discussion on the subject of feminism with some degree of confidence.

THE PROBLEM

Feminism is becoming an increasingly accepted part of ordinary social and political discourse, even if it is not viewed in the same light by everyone. However, feminism now, as in the past, entails a variety of widely differing approaches. And yet, in spite of this diversity, feminism is often represented in everyday discussions, as well as in lecture rooms, as a single entity and somehow concerned with 'equality'. This limited portrayal is rarely challenged, partly because many forms of current feminist analysis require considerable previous knowledge and are sometimes only available in forms of academic language so difficult that they make Einstein's theory of relativity look like a piece of cake. Contemporary feminist thought has sometimes, in this context, been accused of retreating from broadly understandable language into an incomprehensible jargon typically associated with 'ivory tower' academics.[2]

Whether this accusation is fair or not, the problem remains that despite a growing awareness of and potential audience for feminist ideas, feminist thought is little understood—even among academics. I have been lecturing in the field of feminist thought for well over a decade and have recently been struck by the ever increasing number of students and staff from other courses and disciplines asking me for assistance. It is both a pleasing and dispiriting development. On the one hand, academic teachers wish to include some reference to feminist approaches in their subjects and, relatedly, students are now often required or wish to write on topics involving women, 'gender' issues, bodies, sexuality, et cetera. On the other hand, teachers within universities and in other settings find that it is no simple matter to gather together the resources necessary for even the most basic inclusion of contemporary feminist frameworks in their subjects. And students ask for assistance because, while there may be some discussion of feminism in the courses they undertake, the material provided typically either assumes feminism is equivalent to (North American) liberal feminism or hints gloomily at the hardships involved in coming to grips with contemporary feminist thought without much further clarification. The problems associated with gain-ing some understanding of the term 'feminism' are usually even greater for those outside educational institutions. In this context, teachers, students and other interested individuals obviously require some reasonably quick, painless and relatively straightforward guide through the complexity of the field.

A close look at the range of materials commonly employed by teachers attending to feminism goes some way to explaining why it is actually quite difficult to gain a satisfactory grasp of the field. Although feminist thought has been considered by many authors, existing writers rarely attend to the issue of what it is they are discussing. The meaning of the term 'feminism' is almost invariably assumed and/or evaded. Furthermore, most texts dealing with contemporary Western feminism tend to deal only with some aspects of feminism—such as focusing on more established ('modernist') approaches, or only summarising various 'types' of thought named feminist (which does not explain why they are so named). The result is that those who hope to become better informed about feminism have little choice but to struggle through several texts and try to develop some perspective of their own.

While I do not for one moment suggest that wide reading or the process of attempting to figure out the characteristics of a field of knowledge are undesirable, there is no doubt that most of us face restrictions on the time and energy necessary to devote to these forms of intellectual preparation. Moreover, I see no reason why finding out about feminist thought has to be such a chore. On these grounds there seemed to me a definite place for a book which provides a reasonably accessible analytical guide in one site. This book is not supposed to replace wider reading but it is intended to make that reading more efficient and less agonising.

The book clarifies the question of what contemporary Western feminism involves and thus offers a 'definition' of the term. The notion of 'defining' feminism is controversial.[1] In addition to the problems associated with a complex, shifting and sometimes inaccessible field, defining feminism also involves considering whether it is in any sense distinguishable from 'other' forms of thought. As will be noted shortly, the issue of feminism's 'borders' is a matter of debate. Finally, feminists themselves often indicate considerable reluctance to engage in the task of definition. In the main, feminists are inclined—frequently deliberately—not to define what they mean by feminism, sensing dangers such as internal policing of both the field and of feminists by those who might like to determine what is to be included (or not), as well as the potential danger of constricting the unstable vitality of its meanings.

Although the problems associated with defining feminism are inclined to make one pause, I believe that discussion about the meanings of the term is not to be dismissed because it is an arduous undertaking. It can also be argued that refusing to engage in definition does not mean that the question of definition is avoided, rather it leaves implicit definitions in place. These problems in my view indicate that greater attention needs to be paid to *how* the task of definition might be approached. Nevertheless, any brief, neat account of feminism is likely to be disputed. The 'definition' provided in the book is inevitably rather more of an exposition or 'map'. In common with Braidotti,[4] I consider that feminism's manifold qualities suggest a cautious, open-ended and wide-ranging approach to exploring its characteristics rather than an attempt to find some concise central core. Shortly I will explain how I understand the task of 'defining' in more depth but, for the moment, what is relevant here is that such a map or guide is inevitably far more fluid and extensive than any fixed definition that you might find in a dictionary or encyclopedia.[5]

Unlike dictionary definitions, this 'mapping' methodology encourages tendencies to write at great length and in painstaking detail. I was determined to resist such tendencies. I wanted to write more of a pocket-book analytical guide rather than a full-blown overview text in order to assist those who require a quickly absorbed but comprehensive reference, and for this to be of use to a wide variety of readers.

My reason for writing such a book is that an answer to the question of what makes a particular group of writers **feminist** theorists—rather than some other sort—is not as obvious as you might imagine. Although I think there is reason to be wary of strict definition in the traditional dictionary sense, feminism is not a term that is entirely up for grabs. As Rothfield notes, feminism is scarcely a static label, but '[t]his is not to suggest that feminism has no boundaries'.[6] The use of words or labels (no matter how broadly and conditionally understood) does involve the inclusion of something(s) and the exclusion of others, even if the boundaries change over time and are permeable or fluid rather than concrete. Hence, it becomes important for those who wish to understand a term to explore *how* the term may be 'defined'. Because a term like feminism means something(s) and not others at any given moment in time, in a cultural climate where the term is in common usage, the problem of defining or characterising feminism takes on a measure of urgency.

As I have already suggested, there are a number of problems associated with the task of discerning the characteristics of feminism one of which is its variable usage. According to Offen, the term 'feminism' barely existed before the twentieth century. Originating in France, it only began to be employed in the 1890s.[7] In other words, it is a relatively 'new' term within the long history of Western social and political theory and in this sense suggests a new framework or new frameworks. Moreover, its meaning has varied over time and its present multiple meanings are rather different from those in use in the 1890s.[8] **Delmar** suggests in this context that there is no set 'ideal' or vision in feminism. She also distinguishes between the practical politics of the women's movement and a history of ideas.[9] Delmar considers that feminism may exist only in the form of an intellectual tendency with or without the benefit of a social movement. However, many feminist writers do not accept a conception of feminism as simply a set of ideas existing in the absence of a movement. In other words, there are both broad and narrow definitions of feminism which affect how you see feminist thought and what it might be said to offer.

Delmar notes that in contrast to this lack of uniformity in response to the question of 'what is feminism?', there has often been a considerable degree of consistency in the images said to represent feminism and feminists.[10] When you consider that images may refer to styles of dress, haircuts, ways of behaving, attitudes and so on, you can probably conjure up a number of graphic pictures yourself. It is interesting that these easily evoked images are more often associated with pejorative views of feminism. However, the images also suggest an impulse to tie feminism down to something and to ignore considerable differences over the characteristics of feminism.

APPROACH AND ORGANISATION

Perhaps one way of dealing with the difficult task of establishing 'what is feminism?' is simply to avoid trying to arrive at a clear-cut definition, to cast off a notion of burrowing ever-inwards towards a definitive core. After all, there is no reason why characterising or defining a term is necessarily to be equated with discovering its supposed eternal essence. Instead, given the purpose of this book and its focus on feminist theory, definition becomes a more modest task, 'a clarifying device'.[11] Accordingly, I have adopted a method which involves looking at the task of 'definition' from various perspectives and am more concerned to provide the sense of a field alive with possibilities than with locating a tidy answer.

In Part I (chapters 1 and 2) I look at the relationship between Western feminist thought and 'traditional' Western social and political thought. This section, entitled 'Departing from traditional fare', provides the first taste of how feminism may be regarded as diverging from the 'diet' of mainstream thinking. In other words, I start the process of 'defining' feminism from considering that which various feminists describe as providing a point of 'departure'. Feminists indicate what they mean by the term as they point out what distinguishes it from 'other' (non-feminist) bodies of thought. However, it must be noted at this juncture that aspects of those bodies of thought supposedly 'outside' feminism are nonetheless incorporated into feminism.[12] This raises certain issues. If even some feminists include 'within' feminism aspects of that which they have demarcated as non-feminist, how then is feminism in any sense distinguishable from these other forms of thought?

It appears that feminism has boundaries (feminism does

involve some distinguishable meanings) but, at the same time, the interchanges between feminist thought and 'other' forms of thinking which feminists criticise indicate that there is unlikely to be a strict, clear-cut dividing line between them. Perhaps the image of the Berlin Wall is helpful in illustrating this seeming inconsistency. The Wall no longer provides a physical barrier—it is continuously breached—and yet this does not mean that East and West Germany are indistinguishable. Similarly, feminism has boundaries which may be permeable, but this scarcely implies that feminism is no different from any other form of thinking. Rather, the issue becomes not simply where feminism's boundaries might be, but how they might be understood. As a result, clarifying boundaries (how feminism departs from 'other' bodies of thought) and their potential permeability (the ambiguities of that departure), are both part of the first steps in 'defining' feminism.

Part II, 'Active ingredients', allows the reader to digest feminism's volatile dimensions, to absorb the character of its 'cuisine'. Thus, by contrast with the first section, part II begins to depict the parameters of feminism from a standpoint designated by feminists as 'within' feminism. This leads, in chapters 3 and 4, to overviews of the field. (The discussion outlined here is subject to the same concerns regarding boundaries as those noted earlier.) Finally, chapters 5 to 8 offer brief descriptions of most of the generally agreed 'dishes' available on the menu of Western feminism, providing an opportunity to partake of its several varieties.

The intention of the book's organisation is first to outline how feminism is distinguished from 'other' forms of thought—that is, the implications of negative demarcation (Part I)—and, second, to delineate the field in a number of ways, that is, marking out both the dimensions and content of a positive terrain (Parts II and III). This yields a workable, if rather pragmatic, analytical guide to the problem of 'defining' feminism. A pragmatic guide allows for diversity and change as well as indicating potential difficulties attached to overly rigid or clear-cut definitions which attempt to lay down the law regarding what is and what is not 'feminist' thought.

Because the task of 'definition' is pursued pragmatically, the assertion of my own views is restricted to the proposal about *how* to characterise feminism and I have tried to avoid being prescriptive when surveying the content of that field. Throughout the book I intentionally do not engage with the different strands of feminism or with different writers in the sense of offering evaluative comments, in order to leave the field as open-ended as possible. The aim of this less judgmental style is both to forgo the suggestion that I can discern the real, best or essential feminism and to allow you, the reader, to consider this for yourself. However, my concern to avoid an overly prescriptive tone also reflects a point of view in relation to the various 'types' of feminism. While I am presently pre-occupied with three of these (those described later as psychoanalytic, postmodern/poststructuralist and those attending to race/ethnicity), I am able to see uses for all the types of feminism in certain contexts and hence do not regard myself as entirely committed to any one of them.

This description of the book's organisation also reveals two coexistent elements: first, various ways of understanding the term, feminism, are indicated and some schematic considerations and parameters are arrived at which amount to a proposal regarding a 'definition' or map of the field; second, in the process an overview of the content of the field is also provided. In other words, the book contains both **argument** and **survey**.

There are two further points to make in terms of the presentation and structure of the book. Initially, readers will discover that the characterisation of feminism and feminist thought begins in a quite accessible fashion but in general becomes progressively more demanding. This is because, as the 'types' of feminist thinking are described, the material to be covered becomes for the most part less widely understood. Some descriptions refer to exacting bodies of thought outlined in very condensed form.

In addition, there are certain self-imposed limits on the task of characterising feminism undertaken in this book. Such limits include a focus on Western feminisms, and a focus on theory. With regard to the initial caveat, this book specifically provides a guide to Western feminisms as I do not believe that it would be a simple task to provide a short but comprehensive account of both the diverse field of Western feminist thought and the enormous complexity of 'Third World' feminist thinking. I wish to focus on the former with some reference to possible points of interconnection.

In relation to the second self-imposed limit, the book examines the meanings attached to the term, feminism, from the point of view of a focus on feminist theory and thought and feminist theorists—that is, it deals in ideas, assumptions and frameworks. Some writers adopt the view that feminism should not be conceived in terms of ideas alone, since it also refers to political struggles. Others suggest feminism could be described even more broadly. Braidotti, for instance, talks of 'the means chosen by certain women to situate themselves in reality so as to redesign their "feminine" condition'.[13] While I have considerable sympathy for this expanded scope, this book was written to provide a relatively short analytical guide which concentrates on systemic, publicly asserted feminist ideas—rather than on the historical development of feminist political movements, practical struggles, feminist sub-fields or modes of inquiry such as economics or cultural studies, or individual women's negotiation of the 'feminine'. Given my earlier mention of the issue of broad or narrow definitions, it is important to note that I have undertaken an account of feminism and feminist thought which is expediently but necessarily restricted. In any case, I suspect that the apparently limited focus on ideas will give you, the reader, plenty to go on with.

Part I   Departing from traditional fare

1

Feminism's critique of traditional social and political thought

Feminist thinkers regard feminism as somehow different from the mainstream—as innovative, inventive and rebellious. In particular, they see their work as attending to the significance of sexual perspectives in modes of thought and offering a challenge to masculine bias. From the point of view of feminist writers, 'traditional' or 'mainstream' Western thought (which includes a wide variety of thinkers from Plato and Hobbes to Sartre and Habermas)[1] is better described as '**male**stream' thinking and thus its authority needs to be questioned.[2] What does feminism's perceived departure from and defiant stance in relation to traditional thought amount to? I will attempt in this chapter to outline some broad parameters concerning what constitutes feminism by indicating how feminists of various sorts criticise mainstream viewpoints and hence in the process distinguish specifically feminist approaches.

FEMINISM AND THE CRITIQUE OF MISOGYNY

In the first instance it is evident that feminist theories and commentaries upon traditional thought have developed in parallel with mainstream social and political thought. They have in fact developed at something of a remove from mainstream thought. One way of exemplifying this remove is to look at the nature of the content of academic journals, the life-blood of publicly available academic intellectual debate. Current journals which discuss social and political thought tend to discuss a canon of major male theorists and are usually dominated by male writers, with few references to women theorists, feminist analysis or to women's position in social and political life. By contrast, journals which might be called feminist are dominated by women writers who regularly discuss classical and contemporary male theorists' views.[3] The flow of ideas in academic journals is definitely one way. It exemplifies what is, for the most part, a one-sided interaction between feminist and mainstream theory and theorists. Yet, ironically, feminist writers are the ones who are typically perceived as interested in an overly specialised field without 'broader' applications and marked by sexual separatism.[4]

Mainstream social and political theory today is characteristically generated at a distance from feminist thought. However, feminists have argued that this is simply a part of three on-going processes: excluding, marginalising and trivialising women and their accounts of social and political life. (Trivialising occurs when women's experiences are reinterpreted in terms of those associated with men,[5] when feminist writers are said not to talk about the 'big' issues, or when feminist writers are shown 'respect' in a patronising way.)

What clearly links 'feminist' as against other theoretical frameworks, it would seem, is a particular view of traditional social and political thought. That view involves a critique. It is a critique of misogyny, the assumption of male superiority and centrality. As Theile says, '[i]t is common knowledge among feminists that social and political theory was, and for the most part still is, written by men, for men and about men'.[6]

FEMINIST RESPONSES TO MISOGYNY

Though feminist accounts offer a critique of mainstream thought, there have been several different feminist responses to the perceived inadequacy of that thought. I will briefly outline a number of important responses. The first response involves a view that women and women theorists have been omitted from Western social and political theory and that therefore the task of feminist thinkers is to put them back in (while leaving most of traditional thought relatively intact). This might be described as the **'inclusion/addition'** approach, otherwise known as 'add Mary Wollstonecraft and stir'.[7] The emphasis here is on pragmatic concerns related to reforming Western thought taking into account what is politically possible.

The second view declares that, as Clark and Lange put it, 'traditional political theory is utterly bankrupt in the light of present [feminist] perspectives'.[8] This is the **'critique, reject and start again'** or the 'go back to the drawing board' approach. Such an approach expresses doubts about the success of any agenda to 'fix' traditional thought since that thought is conceived as built upon assumptions regarding sexual hierarchy.

Finally, there is the view that it would be impossible to develop a theoretical framework completely uncontaminated by past perspectives or by the history of male domination.[9] Such a perspective argues that we cannot escape our social and intellectual context and, ironically, that traditional thought might be seen as a means to elaborate feminist theory itself, since the more we understand the sexual politics of our cultural and intellectual heritage the better able we are to comment on and transform it. Feminist thought is here regarded as revealing the partial and sexualised character of existing theoretical knowledges. This is the **'deconstruct and transform'** approach. If traditional thought is seen as a woollen sweater, the above viewpoint might be described in the following terms: 'don't throw away the wool, but rather unravel and restitch the jumper, perhaps several times'.

CHALLENGING WOMEN'S SUBORDINATE STATUS AS SECOND-RATE OR NOT-MAN

I have said that there is considerable agreement among feminists that traditional social and political thought is inadequate, even though they differ over what to do about this inadequacy. Accordingly we may be closer to characterising feminism now because some general agreement in perspective if not in strategy can be detected. Moreover, there is general agreement over *what* is inadequate about traditional social and political theory. In other words there is also agreement about flaws in the content of traditional thought. The South African feminist Bernadette Mosala perhaps sums up the basis of the consensus about that content when she says of mainstream thought, 'When men are oppressed, it's tragedy. When women are oppressed, it's tradition'.[10]

Feminist writers regularly point out that mainstream social and political thought has commonly accepted and confirmed women's subordinate position in social and political life, either explicitly or implicitly.[11] Feminists argue that mainstream theory largely takes for granted women's subordination and assumes that this is not a centrally significant topic of political thinking. Whether or not the various forms of mainstream thought express a progressive concern with emancipation, equality and rights, they all tend to accept that women's position is to be taken as given, at most viewing it as of relatively marginal interest. According to Porter, there appear to have been two major ways in which women's accepted subordinate status has been explicitly presented in mainstream thought.[12]

The first view involves an account of women as **partial helpmates**. Here women are defined in terms of men's needs regarding pleasure, provision of services, children and so on. Such a perspective is particularly evident in Judaeo–Christian theology[13] and Greek philosophy, both of which remain fundamentally important in present-day Western political concepts as well as in the general cultural heritage of the West. One example of this account of women may be found in the work of Aristotle. He argued that while the 'rational soul' is 'not present at all in a slave, in a female it is inoperative, [and] in a child undeveloped'.[14] Aristotle linked 'rationality' to ethical virtues (moral qualities) and self-control. Women, in his view, are therefore in need of care and control and are morally unstable. Another example may be found in the work of St Augustine. St Augustine asserted that only man is in the image of God. Women were partial beings for St Augustine because he linked God's image with a particular view of reason.[15] Women's lesser spiritual and social status is a consequence of their link to sensuality and nature, while men are committed to reason and authority. Once again women can only be cast as assistants, given their intrinsic failings and limitations. This notion of women as partial beings, and as *for* men, constituted women as second-rate, as flawed or blemished men. Such a view is still evident in much of Western thought today.

Secondly, feminists found in mainstream thought a conception of women as **different but complementary**.[16] Supposedly in this account both sexes are valued. However, in practice women are described not just as different but as men's opposite. Women, in other words, are defined not so much as *for* men but as *in relation to* men. Man is the norm and woman is defined negatively in relation to that norm. Man becomes the standard model and woman the creature with extra and/or missing bits. (The alternate view, in which women are seen as the starting point, is expunged—even though this perspective is just as possible.) The notion of man as the norm is certainly a view alive and well today. For example, a person who cannot become pregnant (a man) is the standard worker of industrial law in Western countries. Women—people who may become pregnant—are not the general reference point but rather represent a particular group with special (and problematic) requirements. Simone de Beauvoir summed up the hierarchical relationship between men and women assumed in the concept of 'different but complementary' in these terms: 'He is the subject, he is the Absolute—she is the *Other*' [emphasis added].[17] Woman is not so much second-rate man in this context as that which is 'not man'.

Woman becomes a kind of rag-bag of repressed elements that cannot be allowed within the masculine. Hence, women come to represent physical reproduction and the nurturing of dependent children within industrial law, even though men in the workforce have children too. Once again in the 'different but complementary' approach men are linked to rationality, to civilisation, to the 'big picture' beyond specialised small-scale concerns, and to what is particularly human (rather than merely animal). By contrast women are associated with the non-rational or irrational, with the supposedly narrow concerns of kin, and with biology and nature. Any notion of overlap between or uncertainties in the meaning of terms like 'rational' and 'emotional' is precluded or discouraged. An example of this kind of approach in traditional thought occurs in the work of Rousseau, who opposed those who saw women as flawed men. By contrast, Rousseau saw the sexes as different kinds of beings. He considered that women should be educated to please and complement men.[18] Women's difference, appropriately directed, was to be viewed as for men's benefit.

Both versions of women within traditional social and political thought do not allow women much capacity or room for analytical ('rational') thinking. Women are defined as precluded from theorising. What they 'think' is either not on the agenda at all or is seen as being of little significance. Women are not the subjects of social or political thought, nor are they seen as being capable of engaging with it or contributing to it. If you have ever wondered why many women are inclined to think abstract intellectual theorising has not much to do with them, it may be because in a very real sense it has not.[19]

In this setting the book you are now reading itself involves a kind of subversion of or challenge to mainstream social and political thought. Women are at the centre of the theories discussed here and are also construed as theorists. Women are both the subject and the agents (active practitioners) of theory. This is in keeping with the characteristics of the field which this book investigates, for what unites feminist commentaries on mainstream modes of thought is a critique of the mainstream focus upon men as the centre of the analysis and the related invisibility and marginality of women. Feminist commentators offer a critique of the focus on men insofar as that focus is not recognised. Feminists note that, within Western thought, to speak of men is taken as speaking universally.

FEMINIST CRITICISM OF CLAIMS TO UNIVERSALITY

Feminists consider that a major problem within mainstream Western social and political thought lies in its inclination to universalise experiences associated with men, that is, to represent men's experiences as describing that which is common to all human beings. How is this sleight-of-hand undertaken? Initially contemporary feminist writers often note a characteristic formulation within mainstream theory in which concepts are organised into dualisms (oppositional pairs). Each dualism also contains a hierarchy. Rather than a coupling with equal weight given to both sides, one side of each opposition is represented more positively (as better, more significant) than the other. In other words, traditionally Western thinking is arranged in advance by a series of lop-sided conceptual pairs. Such pairs are so much an accepted principle in our (Western) way of understanding the world that they tend to be instantly recognisable, as is evident in the list below.

However, the reliance of mainstream thought upon paired associations which repetitively represent a hierarchical order is also linked by feminists to an inequitable sexual order. Hence, the characteristic tendency of traditional social and political theory to take men as the central subject of the analysis and extrapolate from their experiences is related to a pregiven conceptual ordering within Western thought. Western thought is organised around pairs of unequally valued associations that mirror over and over again the 'violent hierarchy'[20] of the dualism, man/woman. These pairs of associations are suffused with sexual hierarchy even when apparently at a distance from a concern with sex. Thus certain concepts are aligned with the masculine and placed in opposition to others. The latter are constituted as subordinate to the first order of concepts and are connected with femininity. This may be seen more clearly if we look at some oppositional associations characteristic of Western thinking.[21]

man/woman	freedom/bondage
subject/object	active/passive
culture, society/nature	public/private
human/animal	general, universal/particular
reason/emotion	politics, law, morality/personal,
logic/intuition	familial, biological
selfhood, being/otherness,	presence/absence
non-being	light/dark
independence/dependence	good/evil
autonomy/interconnection,	Adam/Eve
nurture	

On this basis feminists consider that sexual difference actually shapes the intellectual geography of our social and political life. It shapes what we can think and how we can think it. Moreover, by this means, feminists argue, mainstream political thought offers a conceptual schema in which viewpoints associated with men are taken as the view, the standard or rational/sensible/proper, universally applicable view.

The dualistic nature of Western social and political thought means that categories like 'work', 'the public sphere', 'citizen', 'politics', et cetera, become imbued with meanings dependent upon sexual difference and sexual hierarchy. The notion of a link between men, public life and universal ethics (beyond one's own 'particular' interests), and hence greater access to Truth or morality, enables the specific vantage point of men to be seen as the broader picture. Women are then construed as being small-minded, as 'merely' private beings. By a wonderful sleight-of-hand women become magically invisible within traditional social and political theory. It is a sleight-of-hand in two senses. First, women seem to disappear as they are marginalised within the conceptual framework of Western thought. Second, what remains within Western thought is men focusing on themselves. In this latter sense mainstream theory may be seen as a form of masculine self-absorption: the sleight-of-hand amounts to another variety of 'hand-job'.

2

Feminism's difference from traditional social and political thought

HOW DIFFERENT IS FEMINISM?

Feminists have not had much difficulty consistently asserting the problematic nature of traditional theory's views of women as either second-rate men or as 'the Other' (not-men). There has not been much dispute among feminists concerning the sexual sub-text of categories like 'the public' or 'the political', nor regarding the problems associated with masculine self-absorption evident in the central focus on 'malestream' thought. Nevertheless, the critique of mainstream Western thought is diverse insofar as feminists are inclined to differ, for example, over *the degree* to which feminism is seen as departing from that thought.

Some feminist commentators argue that the apparent exclusion or marginality of women in traditional theory is simply yet another instance of injustice which just happens to concern women.[1] Feminist social and political thought, according to this point of view, is merely a proposal to *include* women and the relation of the sexes within existing theory. There is nothing special about feminism *per se*. Relations between men and women can be analysed using the same concepts that have been broadly developed in mainstream thought for analysing groups of superiors and inferiors.[2] Feminism is here seen as unremarkable, as part of existing theories concerned with freedom from oppression and *not different in kind* from traditional social and political thought. Feminism's 'disagreement' with the mainstream in this account is more of a complaint about some absences within a mutually acceptable field of endeavour.

By comparison, other feminist writers such as Carole Pateman insist that though women and sexual difference are not acknowledged in social and political theory, they are actually critical to its foundations. In Pateman's view women's marginalised position within social and political thought does not just involve an issue of content, or of omission. Indeed Pateman argues that women's subordination is crucial to the very constitution of the terms of reference, the categories and concepts, and the methods of traditional theory.[3] In this context she considers 'political thought' to be fundamentally constructed out of women's exclusion from the concept—that is, political thought itself is a kind of 'boys' club', run according to game rules assuming a male membership and concerned with activities valued and undertaken by men. This approach asserts that women pose a special problem for traditional theory, since traditional thought is founded on frameworks *dependent* on women's subjugation: for example, commonly accepted frameworks within political theory such as 'the public/private distinction' are built upon notions of a separate, more restricted sphere associated with women. In this viewpoint feminism is seen as differing from traditional thought, as necessarily subversive of the content, assumptions and methods of existing bodies of theory. Relatedly, feminism is considered to be *distinct* from mainstream social and political thought in that feminism recognises women's marginalisation and seeks to overcome it.

However, the question of feminism's difference from traditional thought is not simply an issue about the *degree* of difference. It also raises the problem of how that difference may be understood, or rather how we might interpret feminism's **borders**. Feminists who argue that feminism is not unlike existing bodies of thought appear inclined to perceive interconnections between the two, while those who assert that feminism is positively different might seem more likely to propose clear-cut borders. In practice, although the latter grouping of feminists regard feminism as a challenge to mainstream thinking, they do not necessarily all draw a sharp line between them. Feminism can apparently be envisaged as highly innovative, non-conformist and subversive, and yet simultaneously as integrally intertwined with that which it critiques. In this perspective feminism may be judged distinct but its difference does not necessarily imply isolation from or expunging of 'other' (non-feminist) elements. Accordingly, feminists adopting such a viewpoint may consider feminism as different, even very different from mainstream thinking, but will not perceive that difference—the borders between feminist and 'other' forms of thought—in terms of an impenetrable wall separating irreconcilable antagonists.

As noted in the Introduction, some feminists have drawn attention to the ways in which aspects of those bodies of thought supposedly 'outside' feminism are employed within feminism. For example, feminist thinkers frequently draw directly upon texts imbued with masculine bias in developing their frameworks. Additionally, the project of departing from mainstream (masculinist) thought suggests a necessary familiarity with and active usage of that knowledge.[4] On this basis, like a new cuisine, feminism can be viewed as drawing upon older traditions, even using some or most of the same ingredients, and yet offering a definite recognisable shift that is more than a mere reaction to established custom.

In sum, feminists interpret the boundaries between mainstream social and political thought and feminism in two major ways: as a matter concerning the extent of feminism's departure from traditional fare and/or as a question regarding the nature of that departure and hence the form of the boundaries. In the first instance, feminists differ markedly over the degree of departure they envisage, some considering feminism as located upon a continuum shared with traditional thought, while still others perceive a distinguishable difference between them. Second, there is a range of opinion among those who are inclined to the latter view. Some perceive feminism's borders as providing a relatively clear point of separation or moment of revolt, but others interpret these borders as shifting and permeable. In this last account, there is a determination that the notion of borders should not restrict feminism's potential range and directions. However far the departure from the mainstream might lead, it is argued that feminism cannot and ought not be prevented from making 'tactical' use of any mode of thinking, including modes which clearly depend upon masculine bias.[5]

The only 'border', exclusion or limit on feminism's eclectic choices in this approach appears to arise in relation to the meaning of 'tactical' use. Feminism's borders may be permeable in such an approach but, even when these borders certainly do not exclude the mainstream, the term feminism remains associated with a critique of mainstream presuppositions regarding the centrality of *Man* and the related invisibility/marginality of women. Hence, 'tactical' use of the mainstream involves a rejection of its entirety, the totality of its value framework, at the same time as undertaking ongoing engagement with and strategic borrowings from it. In other words, it would seem that feminism is regarded by feminists as at least somewhat different with regard to its content, and by most feminists as also different in kind, from traditional thought. The basis for distinguishing its difference in kind—however this is interpreted—appears to revolve around a refusal of the masculine bias of traditional thinking.

WHAT IS DISTINCTIVE ABOUT FEMINISM?: VIEWPOINTS ON 'SEXUAL DIFFERENCE'

There are obviously a wide variety of feminist views regarding the relationship between feminism and traditional social and political thought. They range from a perspective which considers feminism and mainstream theory to be compatible and quite similar, to an approach which sees feminism as breaking down the very categories that are used in traditional theory. But if, as the latter view suggests, feminism is in some way distinct, what is distinct about it? Feminism certainly does appear, as I have just outlined above, to challenge conceptions of women and sexual difference in traditional thought. However, the critique offered by feminism—that is, the viewpoint that there is something inadequate and unjust about traditional theory—is more straightforwardly encapsulated than what feminism offers as the alternative. What feminism actually offers, beyond its initial criticism of existing thought, is very diverse. And so the question remains, 'what *is* feminism?' How can it be defined from 'the inside' as it were (even if feminism is not always regarded as clearly separable from 'other' modes of thought)?

If we now look briefly at what is understood as constituting feminism—at the alternative it offers compared with viewpoints available within traditional theory—rather than simply looking at the issue of demarcation or feminism's 'boundaries', we might be able to characterise feminism in some general ways. What is the effect of feminism's critique of mainstream thought upon feminism? What does feminism offer that distinguishes it (from traditional theory, for example)? Examining feminism from 'the inside' will not at this point involve an attempt to define feminism by looking at specific feminisms. (The *content* of the term, feminism, will be discussed in more detail in later chapters.) For the moment I simply intend to note some possible broad features that might figure in clarifying what feminism is. In order to do this I suggest looking briefly at the issue of **sexual difference**. Sexual difference is inevitably of some importance in feminism given feminists' inclination to consider the subject of 'women'—a grouping identified by sex differentiation—yet this issue is approached in *at least* five main ways.[6]

(a) Some feminists employ a notion of **sameness**. They assume that men and women are much the **same** and hence are engaged in reworking mainstream theory's conception of woman as defective or second-rate man. These feminists offer an approach in which women are admitted to 'humanity' as described by traditional thought and female oppression is characterised as the restriction of women's human potential. This is a proposal of assimilation. Women are seen as capable of doing what men do, as capable of being 'men' and are expected to enter the world of men. Such an approach has sometimes been described as egalitarian or humanist[7] feminism and is commonly associated with the public face of North American (liberal) feminism.[8] A concern with the notion of sameness is also often linked with liberal feminism generally and with Marxist/socialist feminisms.

(b) Other feminists adhere to the notion of women as distinct, **different** from men, or at least conceive their agenda in relation to women's cultural constitution as different. This perspective involves reworking the conception of the sexes as 'different but complementary'. Such an approach works with the framework of difference but challenges the assumed hierarchy underlying this account of the sexes found in traditional Western social and political thought. By contrast with views found in traditional thought, where women's difference from men is taken as indicative of inferiority, sexual difference is celebrated by these feminists. Such an approach has been called gynocentric feminism.[9] Their agenda may include a concern with separatism, a deliberate choice by women to remain separate from men in some way. The celebration of difference is often associated with (Western) European or 'continental' feminism, though such a position is disputed by many feminists who argue that this typically presents a simplistic divide between French and English speaking feminists and ignores those writers whose work may fit somewhere in between.[10] Attention to the notion of women's difference is also connected most commonly, and less controversially, with radical, psychoanalytic, and 'French' ('écriture feminine' school) feminisms.

(c) An increasing number of disparate feminist writers in the 1990s express concerns regarding any straightforward either/or choice between the 'sameness' and 'difference' viewpoints outlined above, preferring to reject this schema of oppositional alternatives. They **eschew the sameness/difference dichotomy by shifting the focus** of their analysis to **the question of the organisation and effects of power**. While such writers in some senses give more ground to a perspective recognising women's (socially and culturally constituted) 'difference', they are less inclined than the previous grouping to celebrate the strategic or other possibilities of femininity.[11] Rather they downplay the significance of the issue of the similarity or difference between men and women in favour of considering potential strategies which resist or destabilise sexual hierarchy. The accounts of women offered within traditional social and political thought are conceived as providing analytical material to be examined in the process of deciphering power. These writers range from Catharine MacKinnon's emphasis on women's subordination as the consequence of social power, to Joan Scott's interest in moving beyond assumptions concerning fixed sexual categories and her support for 'an equality that rests upon differenc**es**' [emphasis added].[12] Nevertheless, the inclination to eschew the sameness/difference opposition is more likely to be associated with **postmodern/ poststructuralist** feminist work than any other 'type' of feminist thought.

(d) A number of feminist writers make use of a framework of alliance or coalition. Men and women are not so much the same in kind (in an ontological sense) as **potential political allies** and hence can be partners in allied (much the same) struggles. The issue of sexual difference—whether women are like men or not—is viewed through the lens of political struggle. Political struggle and alliance, in relation to sexual or other forms of power, is what produces arenas of similarity and/or connection. On this basis it can be seen as embarking on a reinterpretation of mainstream theory's concern to depict women as flawed men and/or of that theory's account of women as different and inferior. However, this perspective, like the one outlined above, pays limited attention to social and cultural or other comparisons between the supposed characteristics of the sexes. Feminist writers employing such a perspective may possibly perceive women as similar to or different from men but, whatever their views, such writers signal considerable uncertainties about any position which identifies all women as a group. The question of sexual difference is therefore not regarded as a crucial one *in itself*, rather, sexual difference becomes *one* position, among many, for an emphasis upon potential alliances which challenge forms of power. This approach is usually associated with feminists concerned with race/ethnicity[13] but also with some socialist and poststructuralist/postmodernist feminisms. The first two groups are more inclined than the latter to see women as much like men (as potential 'partners in struggle') and to construe specific political alliances between them as more than a temporary, shifting phenomenon.

(e) Finally, certain feminists consider women to be morally superior to men, to be **better** than men. This approach involves an inversion, rather than reworking, of the mainstream conception of the sexes as different but complementary. In this case the hierarchical relationship between the sexes assumed to be associated with sexual difference in mainstream theory is turned upside down. The notion of women as better people is often (though not always) connected to a perception of women as *innately*, intrinsically pre-eminent. Women's inherent advantage may be viewed as being derived from their special moral–ethical make-up, the specific qualities of their bodies and/or the particularity of their shared experience. Such an approach is particularly associated with radical feminism and is likely to be influenced by the North American 1960s/70s antecedents of this form of Western feminism.

CONSIDERING WOMEN AS THE SUBJECT OF THE ANALYSIS

The variety within feminism simply in relation to the issue of sexual difference indicates that a range of alternatives to traditional social and political thought may be offered by feminist theory. Moreover, this variety implies a number of very different contents for feminism, as well as an array of different sorts of political strategies associated with feminism. Once again what is specific to feminism is somewhat unclear. Can feminism be distinguished as anything more than a mere list of frameworks called feminisms, which are so described only because they are critical of conceptions of women and sexual difference in traditional Western thought? Can feminism only be defined negatively and as a mere menu of complaints concerning injustice towards women? Even from the brief illustration of responses to sexual difference, it would appear that some further clarification might be possible. What does seem to be a feature of all these existing feminisms is the **consideration of women as the subject**: women are at the centre of the analysis. This is not to suggest that feminism is necessarily identified exclusively with women[14] but, as Delmar notes, **the concept of 'womanhood' is placed centre stage,**[15] even when this concept refers to multiple differences, is distanced from any singular content and/or is distanced from any set content such that it is destabilised.

The process of locating women as the subject rests upon a critique of conventional notions of male superiority and centrality, but the repositioning of women and the critical context for that repositioning both generate analytical possibilities. This new content, focus and orientation within feminist thought (new in terms of mainstream Western thought) is accompanied by an expanded definition of what may be described as 'politics' or 'social' life, an expanded definition of what is to be examined. For example, the domestic, the private realm, bodies, sexuality, emotionality, and children are brought into the analysis, in a move that is appropriately summarised by the slogan, 'the personal is political'.

The limits of social and political thought are shifted and hence new arenas for study come into play. In the process 'Man', the subject of traditional thought, is also inevitably reassessed. Accordingly, the term feminism may be seen as including certain positive and indeed creative characteristics, as well as negative parameters, in its definition.

Despite the significance of this reconsideration of women as the subject of theoretical analysis, of the question of 'womanhood', there is surprisingly little consensus within feminism about what womanhood is or might be. Delmar notes in this context that feminists have never agreed about the concept of womanhood. Indeed some contemporary feminists (such as those concerned with issues of race/ethnicity and/or influenced by poststructuralism/postmodernism) are inclined to reject any singular account of the concept because it does not note differences between women or are suspicious of any such concept.[16] However, the seeming instability of the concept may not undermine its critical status for feminists and may signal a fruitful indeterminacy characteristic of feminism.[17] So what then is feminism and what does it presently offer?

CRITIQUE OF SEXUAL HIERARCHY, CONSIDERATION OF WOMEN AS THE SUBJECT, PLUS DIVERSITY

Delmar asserts that the early women's liberation movement of the 1960s and 1970s largely lacked a developed theoretical approach. Hence the movement could assert without much detailed analysis a notion of unity among women and regard 'feminism' as a framework which reflected that unity. She argues that as feminist thought developed it displayed a concern with building on this notion of unity and attempted to find causes or even a single cause of women's oppression. The intention was to find an explanation for women's oppression which would express women's commonality and thus bind all women together politically. If all women were oppressed by the same thing(s), then feminist theory would be the means to demonstrate the notion of a unified womanhood and the requirement for a common political agenda. Ironically, as feminist thought became ever more elaborate the tensions created by this monolithic approach became evident and feminism's supposedly unified front broke openly into disputes.[18]

Whether or not Delmar's point of view is accepted, feminism is now increasingly marked by very diverse accounts outlining different conditions and contexts for particular women in recognition of **differences between women**. Additionally, the search for a unifying cause or causes of women's subordination has become less fashionable. While feminist thought may be broadly defined by its critique of traditional social and political theory and its related consideration of women as the subject of theoretical analysis, 'womanhood' is by no means inevitably viewed as a unified subject. This plurality may itself be just a fashion in feminist thought (though I somehow doubt that differences between women can now be ignored), but the current stress on diversity does complicate answering the question, 'what is feminism?'.

Is diversity itself a distinguishing feature of feminism? Perhaps feminist thought may be 'defined' only in some minimalist sense by its critique of sexual hierarchy—of male dominance—and its related engagement with the question of

20

'womanhood' (however that question is conceived). But, is this a sufficiently detailed or an adequate description of the range of feminisms which exist? More importantly, whether or not diversity is an inevitable element in the feminist 'package', the question remains, 'is that variety without limit?'. The issue of 'boundaries' mentioned at the beginning of the chapter recurs. It is possible that the difficulties which arise in this search for something distinctive, something definable, about feminism—and relatedly for some limits/boundaries—may reveal that the search itself is no longer important or meaningful. Does the process of characterising feminism necessarily assume or demand a unity that feminism has never had and does not need?[19] On the other hand, if feminism's distinctive characteristics are *so* unimportant or insubstantial—its diversity so limitless or ineffable—perhaps the label itself should be abandoned? Yet such a manoeuvre might return us to the discredited clutches of traditional thought.

These issues are by no means easily resolved. Nonetheless, the term, feminism, does appear to offer more than a merely negative or reactive criticism of mainstream thinking. Indeed, feminism would be a peculiarly empty terminology, a critical stance without a critique, if it were so limitless that it could not be somewhat more specifically characterised. In this context, I suggest that the precarious project of delineating feminism's characteristics cannot be entirely evaded. As Thompson notes, '[r]efusing to engage in definition does not mean that definition is thereby avoided altogether'. Reluctance to clarify explicitly the meaning(s) of feminism—no matter how theoretically principled—has the effect of leaving in place implicit knowledges[20] which in my view tend to be largely available to 'those in the know'. Implicit knowledges are inclined to preserve the authority of an already informed elite and make the complexity of feminist thought inaccessible to the broader community. Hence, while the task of defining feminism is a controversial and difficult one, plagued by many problems, it is also both unavoidable and risky to attempt avoidance by omission.[21] And in any case perhaps we should not be too precious about the dangers of pinning feminism down. The assumption that clarifying the meanings of feminism

inevitably requires a prescriptive search for unity, for a definitive, unshakeable core, rather prejudges the task of 'definition'.

As I noted in the Introduction, there is no reason why
characterising or defining a term must be equated with a quest
for a central unity, a fixed central sameness. When definition
is conceived more modestly as being limited to clarification of
existing parameters which are unlikely to mesh into some neat
overall whole, the issue of what might distinguish feminism
becomes less final and more open. Given that we are able to
talk about feminism and feminist thought (thinkers) at all, it
would seem we are referring to and implicitly 'defining' some-
thing(s). This implies that feminism's diversity is not limitless,
but not that these distinguishing elements are necessarily per-
manently or intrinsically fixed or subject to invariable
interpretation. Certainly those who feel they do not understand
the term and wish to learn more about it are likely to be
excluded from debates about the meaning of feminism if there
is *no* attempt to clarify how it might be presently characterised.
But this concern to clarify does not need to invoke a narrow
conception of 'definition' which reduces the meanings attached
to feminism by only recognising what is supposedly always the
same within feminist writings. Some further analysis of the
problems that arise when considering what feminism's distinctive characteristics might be is appropriate at this juncture.

Part II   Active ingredients

3

Debates 'within' feminism about feminism

Having discussed the question, 'what is feminism and feminist theory?', largely from the perspective of a comparison with 'other' bodies of thought—that is, from the 'outside' looking in or from the negative viewpoint of feminism's boundaries—this chapter will attempt some further clarification by giving greater attention to feminism's 'internal' characteristics. Feminists, as noted earlier, do not always consider feminism to be clearly separable from 'other' modes of thought, but limiting analysis of the term solely to how it might be compared with and demarcated from 'other' modes does seem to imply that feminism is inevitably just reactive and lacks 'autonomous' creativity. On this ground, it is useful to signal feminism's dimensions as a *positive* terrain. As the two previous chapters have suggested, there is no simple way of presenting what feminism *is*. I have already given some broad indications of these dimensions, but more detail is likely to be helpful. In Part II the focus on 'internal' debates in feminism will be followed by a listing of elements and broad 'overviews' of the field. (The debates are intended to raise points of dispute concerning feminism's dimensions, while the listing and overviews attempt to summarise discussion of these dimensions.) Finally, an account of the diversity of feminism's content is provided in Part III. The aim of these different strategies in the two Parts is to offer several tastes of the ingredients in this volatile cocktail.

FEMINISM BY THE BOOK: DICTIONARY AND OTHER CONCISE DEFINITIONS

Clarifying the meaning of feminism is often undertaken by referring readers to a number of concise definitions, some dictionary-based. These can be handy because they are short, to the point and easily quotable. Hence they have the great advantage that if someone quizzes you about the nature of feminism, you can appear confidently knowledgeable instead of shuffling your feet and mumbling incoherently. Nevertheless, brief statements of definition do tend to reduce the subtle complexity of a messy field of knowledge to neat slogans. Precisely because these statements are clear-cut and concise they are of limited value if you want to grasp the character of the term, feminism, more fully and appreciate its heterogeneous forms. It *is* actually difficult to do justice to feminism when speaking with unequivocal brevity. (I suggest pointing out this paragraph to anyone who thinks you are intellectually precious when you become flustered in response to unsympathetic demands for a plain and pithy definition.)

Statements of definition are worthy of attention however because, apart from providing a ready reply to any enquiries, they refer to some kind of specific content. This indicates that feminism is not generally seen as merely critical of other bodies of thought, or as a mere mode or arena of inquiry. Indeed, more particularly, 'textbook' definitions all imply that feminist thought cannot simply be distinguished by its questioning focus on the concept of womanhood. Feminist theory, at least according to such definitions, has a **normative** quality—that is, it is concerned with what ought not and what ought to exist in social and political life. Feminism appears to offer ethical/moral 'norms' in terms of a critical stance regarding the position of women and envisioning a more desirable state of affairs. It does not have a neutral attitude towards its focus on womanhood. Though feminist thought is often, especially more recently, acknowledged to contain many tendencies or factions, textbook definitions usually evidence a belief that feminism does consist of some (possibly abiding) *values*. The following definitions make this plain.

[T]here are many individual definitions of feminism, and its fundamental meaning is in dispute. Dictionaries usually define it as the advocacy of women's rights based on a belief in the equality of the sexes, and in its broadest use the word refers to everyone who is aware of and seeking to end women's subordination in any way and for any reason . . . Feminism originates in the perception that there is something wrong with society's treatment of women. (*Encyclopedia of Feminism*, 1987[2])

[Feminism] is a doctrine suggesting that women are systematically disadvantaged in modern society and advocating equal opportunities for men and women. (*The Penguin Dictionary of Sociology*, second edition, 1988[3])

There is no political doctrine of feminism *per se*, and the various groups and currents of thought among feminists are often in bitter disagreement. Basically the movement seeks equal political and social rights for women as compared with men. The main common theoretical assumption which is shared by all branches of the movement is that there has been an historical tradition of male exploitation of women. (*The Penguin Dictionary of Politics*, second edition, 1993[4])

[F]or any viewpoint to count as feminist it must believe that women have been oppressed and unjustly treated and that something needs to be done about this. But it does not follow from this that any consensus is available as to the precise forms this oppression or injustice takes, or as to how they should be remedied. (J. Grimshaw, *Feminist Philosophers*, 1986[5])

I adopt a general definition of feminism as a perspective that seeks to eliminate the subordination, oppression, inequalities and injustices women suffer because of their sex. (E. Porter, *Women and Moral Identity*, 1991[6])

It is certainly possible to construct a base-line definition of feminism . . . Many would agree that at the very least a feminist is someone who holds that women suffer discrimination because of their sex, that they have specific needs which remain negated and unsatisfied, and that the satisfaction of these needs would

27

require a radical change . . . in the social, economic and political order. (R. Delmar, 'What is Feminism?'[7])

Dictionary and other concise definitions of feminism clearly presume that all the varieties of feminist thought are perceived to have some common ground—that is, women have had and continue to have a **rough deal** because of their sex. Such an approach strongly implies that feminist thought has some orientation towards group concerns, rather than simply those of individuals. At the very least a 'reluctant **collectivism**'[8] is suggested. However, little more is usually said about this apparently shared content within feminism. Feminists obviously do not concur on why 'the deal' for women was and is rough, whether different women might receive different 'deals' or about what might be done to alter their situation. Concise definitions generally suggest that feminism comprises a constant and common **framework**, a kind of **empty shell** into which may be poured any number of different concerns, details and explanations.

FEMINISM ON UNCERTAIN GROUND?: THE ISSUE OF CHANGING CONTENT

Nevertheless, even this minimalist account of a shared content within feminism has been strongly disputed. Though textbook definitions tend to ignore it, there is some disagreement among feminists as to whether feminism has *any* abiding, unchanging features or values.[9] It is possible to conceive of feminism as simply a critical strategy/stance which is concerned with particular contexts and is short-term in orientation, rather than as the fully-fledged general world-view or doctrine described by dictionaries. In the former version feminism is less a broad (empty shell) framework describing a rough deal(s) for women and more **a question concerning women and power when investigating specific contexts**. Such an account tends towards a provisional content for feminism and depicts feminist thought as **a form of critical endeavour** (at least in the realm of sexual politics and possibly in relation to intersections between diverse forms of power) rather than a particular framework. Certainly feminism is not viewed as offering a specific social analysis or collection of ideas. In this case only a very nominal normative element is conceded, that is, the critical stance undertaken implies an imperative towards change.

Uncertainties concerning an abiding, even if very broad, common ground for feminism appear to be more often expressed in contemporary feminist writings than in the past. Some recent feminist commentaries suggest, in contrast to most current dictionary and other concise definitions of feminism, that because modern Western twentieth century feminism has changed over time it is no simple matter to find a common set of ideas or thread in feminist thought. These uncertainties *sometimes* reflect an associated view that there is a marked divide between the content of feminist thought in the 1960s and 70s and that in the 1980s and 90s.[10] Indeed the notion of an unproblematic, shared content for feminism—a notion largely taken for granted in dictionaries—for a number of contemporary feminist writers is itself rather more a feature of earlier 1960s/70s feminist thought than central to feminism *per se*.

According to this perspective the elements that in concise definitions are usually distinguished as being basic to all feminism are seen as exactly those belonging to an older and therefore specific variety of feminism. For example, feminism is presented in the definitions given earlier not simply as a general framework which assumes that there is 'something wrong with society's treatment of women' (the 'rough deal' scenario), but additionally as a framework containing two common ideas: first, macrosystemic ill-treatment (terms employed include 'subordination', 'oppression' or 'exploitation') suggesting sustained devastating use of power over women and their subsequent victimisation; second, a conception of a desirable alternative involving 'equality', 'equal opportunities', 'equal rights'. Certain contemporary feminist writers have argued that these two ideas, **oppression** and **equality** (in relation to men), are not so much intrinsic to feminism's content as characteristic of Western feminism in the 1960s and 1970s. They assert that beliefs which constitute all women as *victims of oppression* and which propose that women should be *equal to men* (much the same as men) are no longer taken as given by the feminists of the 1980s and 1990s. On this basis many, perhaps most, dictionary and other abbreviated statements concerning the content of feminism could be regarded as dated and as making the error of equating earlier versions of feminist thought with all of feminism.

FEMINISM AS A DISTINCT SOCIAL ANALYSIS/POLITICAL STANCE: REVOLUTIONARY OR ECUMENICAL?

Definitions of feminism that can be found in dictionaries tend to depict a reasonably limited content shared by feminists. Many contemporary feminist writings show marked equivocation regarding this notion of a shared content. Nevertheless, there have always been any number of feminists who have been rather more definite about connecting elements within feminism. While in the contemporary context attention to the diversity of women and their situations has led to doubts about describing feminism as some general perspective capable of being applied to all, at the same time considerable concern has arisen that this focus on diversity might involve abdicating from a recognisable political position. Does an emphasis on the variety of possible positions within feminism mean that feminism is weakened and diluted politically? Does a fragmented feminism lose its 'bite'? In this setting writers like **Bordo** have exhorted feminists not to forget a collective generalised agenda, a shared meaning for feminism: 'too relentless a focus on historical heterogeneity . . . can obscure the trans-historical hierarchical patterns of white, male privilege that have informed the creation of the Western intellectual tradition'.[11] On the other hand, the depiction of feminism as a general doctrine that can speak for all women has become associated with ignoring crucial differences between them—such as cultural differences linked to race/ethnicity—and hence any straightforward notion of a shared set of ideas and values is now contentious.

Clearly ignoring differences is now viewed as a great mistake by contemporary feminists but, as Bordo's comment indicates, this view sometimes sits side by side with an equally strong belief that it is a mistake to understate or refuse any concept of a common content for feminism. In this context **Grant** goes so far as to dispute the amount of attention given to divisions within feminism, arguing that this has led to a common misrepresentation of feminism as 'multicentred and undefinable'. Indeed, according to Grant, feminism has an underlying **foundation**, a foundation developed by 'early radical feminists . . . as the Women's Liberation Movement was breaking away from the largely Marxist Left'.[12]

bell **hooks**, though a writer who deals very specifically with questions of difference, is also most definite about what she sees as the dangers of an overly vague, wishy-washy or simply understated account of feminism's content. She objects to broad inclusive definitions of feminism which give little indication of any particular set of ideas. Indeed, hooks argues that an 'anything goes' approach makes the term feminism practically meaningless. On this basis she rejects the view that 'any woman who wants social equality with men *regardless of her political perspective* . . . can label herself feminist' [emphasis added].[13] hooks, unlike Grant, is not so much preoccupied with pinning feminism down to a particular set of core concepts as she is concerned to exclude what she deems inappropriate to the term. hooks is choosy about what may be called 'feminist' and her answer to the question, 'what is feminism?', involves an identifiable political commitment.

> I think we have to fight the idea that somehow we have to refashion feminism so that it appears not to be revolutionary—so that it appears not to be about struggle . . . I say the minute you begin to oppose patriarchy, you're progressive. If our real agenda is altering patriarchy and sexist oppression, we are talking about a **left, revolutionary movement**.[14] [emphasis added]

In this way hooks sets herself at odds with more broadly-based accounts of feminism in dictionaries and other concise definitions, as well as with those contemporary writers who express uncertainties concerning a shared content for feminism no matter how broadly defined. Moreover, she offers an alternative perspective to those feminists who support linking feminism to a broadly shared content intending that feminism have **broad, even mass, appeal** (such as Naomi **Wolf**[15]), or those that at the very least refuse to deny the label 'feminist' to approaches with which they disagree politically (for instance, the **anti-sectarian** sentiments of Alison **Jaggar**[16]). Finally, hooks' viewpoint concerning the particular political and theoretical character of feminism may be distinguished from those approaches which assume a distinction between feminist politics and theory, thereby allowing for a range of political positions under feminism's broad umbrella. **Davies**, for example, argues that feminism involves a **common broad-based political agenda in contrast to its diverse theoretical beliefs.**[17] For hooks, the political agenda may be shared but there are manifest limits on the extent of political and theoretical diversity that may be termed feminist.

hooks is a clear proponent of the view that feminism is a distinct political stance. Nonetheless, it must be recognised that feminists who value mass appeal, as well as those who merely reject hooks' concern to exclude non-revolutionary political perspectives, may also offer avowed conceptions of feminism as a committed and definitive political stance. Such examples show that, for some feminists, feminism may well represent a specific form of political thinking but it is a more ecumenical politics than hooks would accept. In this context, it is evident that discussions about the nature of feminism are likely to run up against the question of whether its content is intrinsically radical and in the vanguard of social and political thinking, or potentially popularist. Furthermore, the problem of the identity of feminism's politics tends almost invariably to raise a related point concerning the identity of feminism's 'membership'.

SPEAKING OF FEMINISM: MALE FEMINISTS?

There is and has always been much dispute in modern Western feminist thinking about whether feminism is revolutionary in its orientation, and hence likely to be at some distance from popular opinion. 'Are feminists bound to be radicals?' remains an ongoing point of debate in considerations of where or how to draw a distinction between what is and what is not feminism.[18] Intimately connected with this issue is what can and cannot be said and *by whom*. Oddly enough there seems less and less dispute about the latter problem. It would seem that more recently feminism has been defined not simply as a particular framework, set of ideas or social analysis or form of critical questioning around a focus on women and power, but also as representing a **specific body of experience**. This body of experience is taken to refer to the impact of *being* female, *having* a **female body** in Western society. Feminism is not typically perceived to be an unattached disembodied critical approach, range of ideas or politics, it would seem; rather feminism is almost invariably (a) female (discourse). Despite the fact that feminists are increasingly inclined to view womanhood, female identity and female experience as diverse and unstable, notions of an embodied identity and experience are now more than ever placed as necessary to feminism's content, in the sense of defining who is a feminist. Currently a critical aspect of feminism's content appears to be that it is 'spoken' by women. (This is evident even in the work of contemporary feminists who raise uncertainties about the notion of any ready-made shared content for feminism.[19]) While mainstream social and political theory is commonly viewed from within feminism as being male, feminist theory looks more womanish by the minute. As **Delmar** notes,

> In 1866, J.S. **Mill** could be welcomed as an adequate representative of women's aspirations by the first women's suffrage societies. As recently as 1972 Simone **de Beauvoir** could refer to feminists as 'those women or even men who fight to change the position of women, in liaison with and yet outside the class struggle, without totally subordinating that change to a change in society'. Now, in the mid-eighties, it is practically impossible to speak of 'male feminism'. Feminism is increasingly understood by feminists as a way of thinking created by, for, and on behalf of women, as **'gender-specific'**. Women are its subjects, its

enunciators, the creators of its theory, of its practice and of its language.[20] [emphasis added]

In the wake of ever-growing doubts about what, if anything, the category of 'woman' refers to, it is unclear whether this 'intensification of emphasis on women'[21] is possible to sustain. That emphasis renders the question, 'what is feminism?', increasingly dependent on the issue of 'what is woman?', on the conception of a supposedly specific female identity or body of experience distinct from that available to men. Is feminism, despite its diversity, increasingly identified by the concept, woman, such that it is an **embodied theory** and not just a floating framework or set of ideas available to all? But if the category 'woman' is by no means straightforward, how can a clear dividing line be drawn between the sexes? Are men positioned 'outside' of the identity and experience associated with women, which means they *cannot* partake of that which constitutes feminism and hence cannot describe themselves as feminists? Delmar's historical notes on changing views among feminists suggest that although the answer seems generally in the affirmative at this time, it may not remain so.

Additionally, despite the apparent accord on the issue of men's relation to feminism, there are some important dissenting views. Certain feminists concerned with race and/or ethnicity and conceptions of difference, for example, assert that men 'must be part of the feminist movement' or refer to 'male feminists'.[22] In this setting, bell hooks is sharply critical of broad-based accounts of feminism's political orientation but on the other hand includes 'everybody' in feminism's content and membership. This inclusivity is specifically linked to engaging with 'black men in the struggle for their lives' and to challenging crude conceptions of feminism as 'anti-male, anti-family'.[23]

Men may well be included once again under the banner of feminism as feminist theory develops over time (rather than being regarded more in the role of potential barrackers). However, without some recognition of women's social and political positioning as distinct from that of men—that is, some employment of a notion of women as a distinguishable group—it is hard to imagine any meaning for feminism as a theory/politics of change. From this point of view it seems difficult to erase a sexual dividing line of some sort—which brings us back to the possible benefits of a sexually exclusive focus and membership for feminism. While a feminism which examines sexual difference (as well as other differences) but also includes both sexes in its membership is undoubtedly imaginable (as is evident above), the stronger the emphasis on the significance and meaning of a feminine identity and bodily experience in feminist writings the more likely feminism is to be located as a women's movement, as speaking with a woman's voice.

4

Overviews of feminist thought

A SCHEMATIC LISTING OF ELEMENTS

Having outlined some of the debates within contemporary Western feminism concerning its 'internal' characteristics, it seems that the number of relatively uncontroversial elements we might identify as distinguishing the 'diet' of feminist thought is rather small and that even these are neither fixed nor likely to involve only one interpretation. I have suggested that the field of feminism attends to or includes: (1) a critique of misogyny/sexual hierarchy; (2) a focus on consideration of women as the subject of the analysis, which may include references to differences between them and even question the status of the grouping itself; (3) an expanded account of and altered orientation to what may be discussed within analysis of social and political life—compared with traditional thought; (4) diverse perspectives, manifestly represented by certain forms of debate,[1] some of which are described in chapter 3; (5) some recourse to a normative imperative at least in relation to challenging sexual hierarchy (and frequently other intersecting social hierarchies), which may be implicit but more often is clearly evident[2]; (6) some, at least minimal, element of collectivism; (7) an inclination to view feminism as particularly relevant to or resonant with women, though men may also be seen as benefiting from and (by some) as party to its concerns.

However, such an account of the 'cuisine' does not quite seem to summon up my sense of the ever-growing, volatile fluidity I associate with the term, feminism. This plentiful exuberance, so distant from the apparently abstemious frugality of a mere listing of ingredients/dimensions, is not easily susceptible to any form of description. And, more problematically, employment of this listing as a clarifying device to explain the complexity of feminism might suggest an overstated commonality among feminists as well as an overly neat set of 'core' elements for feminism. Many feminists are suspicious when accounts of feminism seem not merely to describe but to prescribe what can be included (and hence what cannot be included) within it. They sense dangers like internal policing of the field and its advocates, as well as the potential to confine the unstable vitality of its meanings. I should make it clear at this point that although a schematic listing of ingredients does contain certain problems, such as the potentiality for prescription in advance, these ingredients are stirred and shaken by various 'cooks'. The 'cuisine' of feminism generates a liberal, indeed intoxicating brew of interpretations.

The parameters outlined above are clearly only relevant to existing feminist work. Their variable interpretation and interaction with one another tends to resist any reduction of feminism to a singular central meaning. Nevertheless, perhaps another approach to the problem is in order. On this basis I will attempt to draw together some of the issues raised in the discussion of 'debates' (chapter 3) and present them visually (Figure 4.1). The initial map can then be employed in conjunction with a more complex visual account of the various feminisms/feminist groupings (Figure 4.2). Together these two rather different pictures are intended to provide a broad *overview* of perspectives on feminism. Such overviews offer another outlook on the question, 'what is feminism?', and can therefore be considered alongside the schematic listing of elements described above. What I am attempting to stress here is that analysis of feminist thought does not simply involve dealing with a plurality of 'types' of feminism—a diverse content[3]—but additionally requires consideration of a plurality of standpoints on how to undertake the analysis—that is, consideration of a range of methodological alternatives.

FEMINISM AS A CONTINUUM: AN INITIAL MAP

Outlining the characteristics of contemporary Western feminism/feminist thought as a 'positive terrain' appears to be a difficult business, even without including much detailed content. While it is extremely useful to be able to provide a generalised overview of feminism's 'internal' dimensions, this is not a simple narrative task. For this reason it is worth attempting to explore the possibilities of an overview in terms of a continuum. On the other hand, any conception of a continuum representing the dimensions of feminist perspectives is limited by its linear emphasis. This emphasis tends to restrict the overview to an account of various responses to a particular—even if broad—aspect of the field. I have chosen to attend to one of the broadest themes within feminism capable of distinguishing among feminist approaches, enabling both some delineation of the scope of the field and some ability to discriminate within it. The continuum attempts to demonstrate the range of responses within feminism to the *question of the definition of feminism itself*. Positions within feminism stretch from those adopting more explicit and specific political commitments which demand less widely inclusive conceptions of feminism's defining qualities, to those stressing flexibility and diversity related to an emphasis upon historical, local and contextual specificity. Feminist approaches are not, however, to be found along the whole length of the continuum presented in Figure 4.1; they are also not to be found at either extremity. Feminists do not apparently hold views of feminism which perceive it as having utterly fixed dimensions or content nor do they regard it as limitless and without any distinguishing features. Though the continuum in Figure 4.1 does not contain a *summary* of the dimensions or content of feminist thought, it can give an indication of its *reach*.[4]

At the left of the continuum we find notions of feminism as a definite set of ideas or social analysis. In this perspective feminist thought can be defined comparatively narrowly and is conceived as a relatively 'closed' approach requiring a commitment to a revolutionary politics which is explicitly collectivist. In the middle of the continuum are broad definitions of

Figure 4.1 Views of feminism's scope

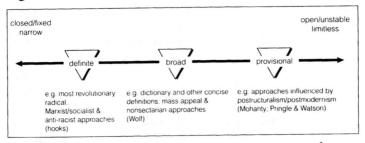

(References here are to hooks[4], Wolf[5], Mohanty, and Pringle and Watson.[6])

feminism, including dictionary and other abbreviated accounts, as well as notions of feminism as either an approach with potentially mass appeal or a non-sectarian collection of ideas or forms of analysis. These broader accounts of feminism are somewhat less likely to attend to political commitment than those described as offering a 'definite' view of feminism's content and, when this commitment is a concern, allow for a wider variety of political positions to be included in what counts as feminist. The effect of this ecumenical breadth is to include positions ranging from those which clearly refer to collective or group concerns to those which largely attend to individual attainment and assume a minimalist approach to collectivism.

The most 'open' definitions of feminism's scope are depicted on the right of the continuum. Here, feminist thought is viewed as having highly contextualised and provisional dimensions or content. Rather than a specific set of ideas or forms of analysis, we encounter approaches that tend to depict feminism as a mode of critical inquiry in the arena of sexual politics, especially politics described in theoretical or intellectual terms. Although there may be some antagonism to binding feminism to a particular politics or ethics, the 'provisional' definitions include many writers whose works make it clear that a feminism which is open to a changing content, and hence rejects a singular political viewpoint, is not necessarily politically promiscuous.

Finally, it is important to recognise that although there are approaches to feminism which may be distinguished by their concern with the provisional nature of feminism's dimensions and content, these same approaches may not be so provisional about the membership of feminism. Indeed of all the positions outlined on the continuum only some within the 'definite' and 'broad' groupings are more 'open' about men being regarded as feminists or being somehow included under the banner of feminism.[5] Characterisations of feminism across the board are more likely to be circumspect about who can speak feminism than about what can be said.

This continuum emphasises the point that when we attempt to define or map feminist theory it is not just a question of merely noting that there are many kinds of feminism. The problem is that there also many differing statements about *which* kinds are to be included and differing explanations regarding *why* these kinds might be included.

FEMINISM AS A PRAGMATIC LIST OF VIEWPOINTS: TODAY'S MENU

The overview continuum demonstrates the lively complexity of the field, the variety of ways in which contemporary Western feminism might be explored. But this initial 'map' provides only a very few signposts and barely hints at the diversity of richly detailed 'landscapes' which await the explorer. Given the difficulty of providing an overall map of feminist thought, I have suggested previously that it may be simpler and more helpful to forgo the desire to see the whole picture. Instead I think there are advantages in laying out several different ways of considering feminism. So far we have examined how feminists demarcate feminism from traditional thought, outlined several broad parameters in that context, depicted some significant debates and provided broad overviews in the form of a listing of elements and a picture of feminism's scope. Another very much more common method for discussing feminism involves a menu of 'types' of feminism. Perhaps it is now possible to define feminism by listing its constituent viewpoints.

Presenting a mere catalogue of the perspectives that have been described as feminist might not seem a very analytically insightful way of characterising feminism and it certainly means that from hereon I adopt without further discussion a most inclusive account. However, if for the purpose of viewing all possible approaches we do not disallow any, definition then becomes a pragmatic exercise, putting to one side agonising about what might be included in the 'best' definition. And so, in order to halt pedantic angst, from here to the end of the book let us be pragmatic. After you have considered all the alternative methods offered in this book for defining or characterising feminism *you* can then decide for yourself which of them singly or in conjunction have been helpful in clarifying the term. Additionally, as you read the accounts of the 'types' of feminism to follow, you may wish to ponder—in the light of the discussion so far—whether or not any of them fit into *your* definition or map of feminism. For now what is important is an awareness of considerable dispute within feminism about the nature of feminist thought.

Feminism or feminist theory defined simply as a pragmatic menu of constituent viewpoints can be viewed as the sum of all the different perspectives described so far, a loose collection with no necessary overarching connection assumed between viewpoints, beyond perhaps broadly interpreted elements listed at the beginning of this chapter. This still leaves much room for debate. Feminist thought is presently in a very fluid state and you, as much as anyone else, can develop an original position or new synthesis of existing approaches. The intention of the remainder of the book is to assist you in clarifying your understanding of, and your own position in relation to, the many different approaches within feminist thought.

THE TERMS OF THE 'PRAGMATIC MENU'—A LIST OF WHAT?

Before a pragmatic list of the varieties of feminism can be presented, there are a few further issues that arise. There is little disagreement among feminists that many kinds of feminist thought exist but feminists have offered widely different accounts of the ways in which they are divided and whether or not these divisions are important. Feminists disagree therefore on how to label themselves, on how to present the different kinds of feminist thought. For example, Karen **Offen** simply divides (Western) feminism into two: **relational** and **individualist**. In the first instance she describes feminists, including feminists prior to the nineteenth century, who have focused on egalitarianism in heterosexual familial settings. 'Relational' feminists, according to Offen, are concerned with a notion of equality which pays attention to women's sex-specific positioning, that is, women's distinct position as women (largely related to child-bearing and nurturing capacities). 'Individualist' feminism, on the other hand, includes a group of feminists who focus upon a quest for personal individual independence and downplay sex-linked qualities.[6]

Elizabeth **Grosz** provides a rather different analysis of the field. She, in common with Offen, divides feminism into two major strands but refers to **equality** and **difference**. Feminists oriented toward 'equality' are described as asserting that women should be able to do what men do. Grosz also employs the term, 'egalitarian feminists' in relation to this grouping and mentions that, for those familiar with more commonly used labels, equality feminism includes liberal (egalitarian) and socialist feminists. Feminists concerned with 'difference' or 'autonomy', on the other hand, recognise and value difference—there being no expectation that women should do what men do. Such feminists support conceptions of difference without hierarchy, difference without a norm, let alone a male norm.[7] Radical, postmodernist/poststructuralist and certain psychoanalytic feminists might be included under this umbrella term.

The work of Offen and Grosz alerts us to the number of ways and the different labels which might describe aspects of Western feminism.[8] In line with earlier comments regarding the advantages of employing a method which is both pragmatic and broadly inclusive, allowing the reader to make decisions regarding definitional niceties, I have chosen a more common and mundane mode of analysis to divide up feminists. Figure

4.2 (see page 48) refers to the various **schools** or **traditions** which enables easy comparisons to be made between the descriptions and interpretations contained both in this book and others. In particular this mode of analysis provides some continuity, and hence points of comparison, with a range of previous overview texts such as those by Jean Bethke **Elshtain**, Alison **Jaggar**, Josephine **Donovan** and Rosemarie **Tong**.[9] These writers employ more extensively dissected accounts of feminism than the comparatively concise two-sided models outlined by Offen and Gross, describing between four to six major feminist approaches. I refer to seven[10]: **liberal, radical, Marxist/socialist, Freudian** and **Lacanian psychoanalytic** (the latter including 'French feminists'), **postmodern/ poststructuralist**, and feminists concerned with **race** and/or **ethnicity**.

THE SCHOOLS/TRADITIONS MODE OF ANALYSIS: SOME PROBLEMS

While the number of feminisms outlined may seem bewildering, some awareness of the schools or traditions is invariably assumed in feminist theoretical writings. All the same it is a categorising approach which has its share of problems, not least of which is the tendency to understate the extent to which individual writers may not fit neatly under one 'label' and/or may change their views over time. In this sense, this methodology might be said to impose a rather too neat order on the typology of feminism and downplay 'cross-overs' in strands of feminist thinking. Or, alternatively, it could be argued that presenting feminism in the form of a list of schools or traditions encourages an overly fragmented picture of feminist theory which obscures an underlying shared core. These are both important criticisms and ones that deserve at least a cursory response clarifying the reasons for adopting such an approach.

In relation to the first concern, Stacey has asserted that a 'category' oriented analysis of feminism may ignore the difficulty that some viewpoints are not so easily distinguished.[11]

Moreover, it can be argued that labelling may discourage the reader from creatively assembling bits and pieces from any combination of or all feminist viewpoints. While I have some sympathy with Stacey's remarks on the problems of labelling and of neat, apparently fixed 'types' of feminism, in my view these problems are only of significance to those already steeped in the field. For those new to feminist theory, guidelines about general patterns are of considerable help. Once some grasp of these patterns has been obtained it might then be appropriate to consider Stacey's important point about the limits of any form of categorisation.

In my work as a teacher of feminist thought I have certainly found it more useful to stress that one can pick and choose aspects of the various feminist viewpoints than to break up the groupings before these are well understood. In other words, the aim of this book is to emphasise the flexibility of the reader rather than focusing on the fluidity of feminist approaches. In my experience, this is a more accessible starting point. In both Figure 4.2 and the commentary to follow, an account of a number of feminist groupings or schools is outlined. These schools are not clear-cut, not all feminist writers fit neatly into only one category and, most importantly, your own views—like those of many within the field—may cross over the groupings.

With regard to the second concern, Grant has stated that presenting the field of feminism as a list of schools or traditions underplays what is shared within feminism and hence involves a prior judgment about the fragmented nature of the field which is both dangerous and misleading.[12] It is evident from earlier discussions (chapter 3) that no account of feminism can ignore those analyses which espouse the notion of a shared content for feminism but, what is regarded as specific to feminism, the extent to which this specificity is held in common in the same way by different feminist writers, and how it is held in common, are contested. Methodologies employed to delineate feminism are certainly required to indicate the possibilities for a shared content, but they cannot be framed by a view that even considering diversity in feminism produces a dubious or inaccurate picture of the field. Just as the issue of shared content is an aspect of feminism, so too are the several 'types' of feminism. Furthermore, it is important that the reader be offered some account of the different versions of feminism since without this knowledge many texts and discussions in the field would be incomprehensible. Nonetheless, it should be kept in mind that for certain feminists like Grant, these 'types' give an appearance of fragmentation which tends to cloud or mask an underlying commonality in feminism. After reading this book it may be helpful to re-assess—in the light of the different criticisms offered by **Stacey** and **Grant** among others—the benefits and limits of characterising feminism in terms of a list of commonly accepted varieties.

COMMENTARY TO FIGURE 4.2

Having decided on how to go about considering the *content* of feminism, it is difficult to outline the many viewpoints that may be included under the term without reducing them to mere slogans and without committing the error of reducing whole traditions or schools to a perspective that may not be held by all theorists in that tradition. Although the various traditions do become more established over time, newer feminist trajectories are often quite messy and are not so straightforwardly summarised. Consequently older traditions or schools in Figure 4.2 are described as 'femin**isms**' and theoretical approaches involving new elements are described in terms of groups of 'femin**ists**'. This distinction is suggested because the latter do not form particularly coherent collections. Attempts to describe such groups in terms of a distinct perspective (as an 'ism') are likely to falter because the description may well fit only some aspects of the work of the writers included in that collection. This problem is especially evident among the so-called 'French feminists' (the 'écriture feminine' school), postmodern/poststructuralist feminists and feminists attending to race/ethnicity. The tendency of more recent feminist writers in particular not to fit comfortably within collective agendas and to retain comparatively idiosyncratic (individualistic?) viewpoints suggests the need for cautious 'labelling'. On this basis it seems appropriate to indicate **group linkages**—loosely formed schools of thought—but not to name still emerging approaches as 'feminisms'. While feminist views concerned with race/ethnicity have been around at least as long as any other type of feminism, I have described them as a grouping rather than an 'ism' because their writings are very diverse, only broadly linked, and include some developing trajectories, such as 'postcolonial' frameworks.

Figure 4.2 offers an overview of the 'pragmatic menu' of contemporary Western feminists/isms and, together with the expanded commentary provided in chapters 5 to 8, it will give an impression of the major schools or kinds of feminism. For those readers with more background in feminist thought, the combination of visual map and commentary will hopefully provide a concise picture of established as well as more heterogeneous, recent, approaches. To assist in 'tasting' the current dishes on the feminist menu, the commentary presented in the following chapters briefly outlines an account of each feminist school and how it is connected to others: a somewhat compressed discussion of the first three feminisms (liberal, radical, Marxist/socialist) and fuller descriptions of the next four (Freudian, Lacanian, postmodern/poststructuralist, race/ethnicity) are given. The disparity in the length of the summaries is because the latter four viewpoints are less widely known. Within this group of four the length of summaries also varies because of differences in their accessibility and the range of knowledges assumed in them. Some are relatively less established in the English speaking world and often draw upon a number of difficult theoretical knowledges. Hence it is difficult to find them summarised in a brief accessible form elsewhere. The outline of postmodern/poststructuralist feminist work is particularly lengthy on this account because of its increasing impact in other feminist approaches.

Finally, as mentioned earlier, this particular presentation (an overview of the content of feminism in terms of seven feminist viewpoints described as traditions or schools) is not the only or inevitable way of characterising this material. It has been a matter of judgment and pragmatic choice, framed by my own teaching. I regard other aspects of Figure 4.2 as more controversial. I refer here to the illustration of 'flows of influence' between various viewpoints. Sometimes a flow of influence is presented as relatively unimportant or non-existent (represented by no connecting arrow), sometimes as largely one-way ($\rightarrow$), and sometimes as involving a degree of mutual interaction ($\leftrightarrow$). My assessment of the existence and extent of links between viewpoints is not crucial to new readers but will probably be of interest to specialists or those wishing to undertake more extensive study in this field.

Figure 4.2 Overview of feminism's content—current feminist viewpoints

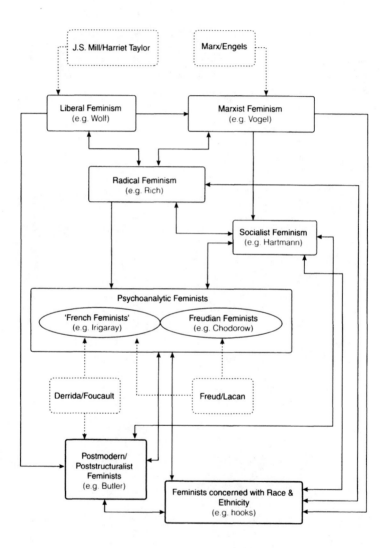

Part III What's on the menu?

5

Starters on the feminist menu: liberal, radical and Marxist/socialist feminisms

A crucial beginning for the different orientations of the several feminisms lies in differences between three major traditions. These traditions, like the ones that have come after them, are not discrete, and many feminists use a little from some or all of them. They are **liberal** feminism, **radical** feminism and **Marxist/socialist** feminism.

LIBERAL FEMINISM

Liberal feminism is the most widely known form of feminist thought and it is often seen as synonymous with feminism *per se*—that is, responses to the question 'what is feminism?' or 'are you a feminist?' commonly draw upon liberal versions of feminist thought. It is certainly the 'moderate' or 'mainstream' face of feminism. In this approach the explanation for women's position in society is seen in terms of **unequal rights** or 'artificial' barriers to women's participation in the public world, beyond the family and household. Thus in liberal feminist thought there is a focus on the **public sphere**, on legal, political and institutional struggles for the rights of **individuals** to compete in the public marketplace. In liberal feminism there is also a critical concern with the value of individual 'autonomy' and 'freedom' from supposedly unwarranted restrictions by others. Though sometimes this freedom from social restraint is understood in terms of freedom from 'interference' by the state or government, more often it is seen as freedom from the bonds of custom or prejudice. Public citizenship and the attainment of **equality with men** in the public arena is central to liberal feminism.

There is a presumption of **sameness** between men and women in liberal feminist thought. Liberal feminist political strategies reflect a conception of a **fundamentally sexually undifferentiated human nature**—that is, since women are much the same as men, women should be able to do what men do.[1] Given an assumed commonality between the sexes and the focus on **access** to what men have in society, liberal feminists do not perceive the sexes to be 'at war' or dismiss that which has been associated with men. Not surprisingly, liberal feminism involves an emphasis upon **reform** of society rather than revolutionary change. A well-known example of this kind of approach may be found in the more recent work of Naomi Wolf.[1] Wolf promulgates what she calls 'power feminism', a feminism based on a sense of entitlement and which embraces monetary and other forms of 'success' in existing society. She explicitly rejects strategies which might be less palatable to 'mainstream' women (and men), effectively dismissing more critical or revolutionary agendas (and is seen by some as offering an increasingly conservative version of liberal feminism). In crude terms, liberal feminists such as Wolf want access to opportunities associated with men. They want what men have got, rather than questioning its value in any thorough sense. This has led to accusations from both other feminists and anti-feminists that liberal feminism suffers from a kind of 'penis envy'. Whether or not this is true it has produced practical benefits for women.

Liberal feminism draws on (but also modifies) **welfare liberalism**[1]—a form of liberal political thought influenced by writers such as J.S. Mill[1]—insofar as this feminist tradition does not challenge the organisation of modern Western societies but rather suggests some **redistribution** of benefits and opportunities. Liberal feminists also take from welfare liberalism a limited acknowledgment of social or collective responsibility, that is, they accept a need for some (possibly government) intervention in the competition between individuals for social opportunities and reject so-called *laissez-faire* liberalism[5] which argues that freedom and justice are best served by nominal government and that a just and natural inequality will emerge if individuals are left to their own devices.

Welfare liberals support certain restricted forms of state intervention on the assumption that, since unregulated inequality may lead to overly harsh social outcomes for some, a society in which inequality is tempered with benevolence towards those who are disadvantaged or less fortunate better advances the welfare of all. Welfare liberals also consider that certain unwarranted barriers hinder the emergence of an authentic merit-based (just and natural) hierarchy. Liberal feminism follows this line of thinking in specifically asserting that women are not fundamentally different to men and yet are denied opportunities on the basis of their sex. Sex therefore constitutes an unwarranted disadvantage, a barrier to competition and the recognition of merit. Hence women's position in society may be the legitimate subject of government intervention.

In this setting liberal feminism provides a framework for the development of 'moderate' feminist policies and practices which can be employed, for example, by government agencies. However, the extent of liberal feminist interest in links with government is very context specific, ranging from the comparatively greater emphasis on individual rights and freedoms—as against connections with the state—in North American liberal feminism to the myriad of interactions between feminists and government to be found in Australia.[6] But, whatever the context, given liberal feminism's concern with working for attainable social change within the existing confines of modern Western societies, it is not surprising that most feminists have perforce made use of this framework.[7] Indeed liberal feminism is the most commonly borrowed—even if only temporarily—approach in the feminist pantheon.

RADICAL FEMINISM

Radical feminism, unlike liberal and Marxist/socialist feminisms, is not drawn directly from previous bodies of 'malestream' thought. It offers a real challenge to and rejection of the liberal orientation towards the public world of men. Indeed it gives a positive value to womanhood rather than supporting a notion of assimilating women into arenas of activity associated with men. Radical feminism pays attention to **women's oppression as women** in a social order dominated by men. According to this approach, the distinguishing character of women's oppression is their oppression as women, not as members of other groups such as their social class. Hence, the explanation for women's oppression is seen as lying in **sexual oppression**. Women are oppressed because of their sex.[8]

That notion of shared oppression is intimately connected with a strong emphasis on the **sisterhood** of women. While differences between women are sometimes—particularly in more recent writings—acknowledged, there is a strategic focus on women's similarities and the pleasures of forming political and other bonds between women in a world where such bonds are marginalised or dismissed. In this context, **Johnson** comments: '[o]ne of the basic tenets of Radical Feminism is that any woman . . . has more in common with any other woman—regardless of class, race, age, ethnic group, nationality—than any woman has with any man'.[9]

Such an agenda encourages some degree of 'separatism' from men, which may range from simply supporting other women to living as far as possible in the exclusive company of women. Furthermore, this identification with women and rejection of male dominance involves both a critique of the existing organisation of heterosexuality as prioritising men and a recognition of lesbianism as a challenge to that priority.[10] Radical feminism stresses that in a social order dominated by men the process of changing sexual oppression must, as a political necessity, involve a focus on women. And because radical feminism recommends putting women first, making them the primary concern, this approach is inclined to accord lesbianism 'an honoured place' as a form of 'mutual recognition between women'.[11]

Sexual oppression is seen as the oldest and even the most profound form of inequality.[12] Radical feminists often view other forms of power—for example, unequal power relations within capitalism—as derived from **patriarchy** (social systems of male domination, the rule of men).[13] Given the significance of patriarchy to radical feminism, it is appropriate to provide a brief account of the term. Although the subject of considerable debate, this term remains widely used and refers to the systemic and/or systematic 'organisation of male supremacy and female subordination'. **Stacey** summarises three major instances of its usage: historical, 'materialist' and psychological. She notes that some feminists employ patriarchy to trace the historical emergence and development of systems of male domination. Others use the term to explore the sexual division of labour (that is, to explore the 'material'—or concrete structural, bodily, physical—aspects of social organisation which divide up and differentially value tasks and activities on the basis of sex). And, finally, certain feminists perceive the term as enabling a recognition of the deep-rooted nature of male dominance in the very formation and organisation of our selves (the psychological or unconscious internalising of social patterns of sexual hierarchy).[14] Radical feminists draw upon all three of these usages of patriarchy as well as others and are among the most committed to its continued employment because of its centrality to their analysis.

Radical feminists adopted an approach in which the recognition of sexual oppression (patriarchy) is crucial, in part at least, as a counter to the politics of the radical left in the 1960s and 1970s which either ignored sexual inequality or deemed it of secondary importance.[15] Radical feminism describes sexual oppression as *the* or at the very least *a* **fundamental form of oppression** (usually the former) and **the primary oppression for women**.[16] Men as a group are considered to be *the* beneficiaries of this systematic and systemic form of power. Radical feminists state the most strongly of all feminist traditions that **men as a group are the 'main enemy'**.[17] In radical feminism all men are unambiguously viewed as having power over at least some women. Indeed this approach commonly suggests that any man is in a position of power relative to all women, and possibly some men.[18] Perhaps the most useful way of summarising this point, to allow for some potential differences within radical feminism, is to state that radical feminists perceive all men without exception as sharing in the benefits of a social system of male supremacy (patriarchy). This 'does not mean that all men are invariably oppressive to all women all the time',[19] nor does this approach deny that some men at least may struggle to overcome this system of domination.

Radical feminism's strong interest in recovering or discovering positive elements in femininity (asserting in essence that it is good to be a woman and to form bonds with other women), in combination with its location of men as the beneficiaries of sexual power relations, results in a relatively sharp division drawn between men and women. In Elizabeth Grosz's terms this is a **feminism of difference**. Radical feminists usually present an historically continuous, clear-cut difference between men and women. Sometimes this is argued to be the result of an ontological (essential, intrinsic, innate) difference.[20] However, other radical feminist writers note that 'male domination is a social structure' and not the consequence of some in-built male propensity, even if motivations towards mastery are 'typically male'.[21] In other words, feminists in this tradition see a difference between men and women as inevitable (given by nature) or at least as so established historically that it is very deeply embedded.

Since radical feminist thinkers consider sexual oppression to be profoundly entrenched, frequently depicting it as the *original* form of coercive power,[22] they also present the social and political changes required to overthrow the system of male domination as far-reaching. As you would expect given the name, radical feminism generally advocates a **revolutionary** model of social change. However, the proposed revolutionary change in the organisation of power relations between the sexes is not described in terms of a single cataclysmic moment, but rather as the consequence of the cumulative effect of many small-scale actions. Moreover, revolutionary practice—conceived as *the* basis of radical feminist theory—is undertaken with an emphasis on small group organisation rather than formalised centrally administered structures.[23]

Radical feminists may pursue a revolutionary agenda but, like liberal feminists, they stress practical political strategies. Nevertheless, in contrast to liberal feminist frameworks, radical feminism is inclined to be suspicious of government intervention, perceiving the state itself as being intrinsically patriarchal, and also tends to focus on the **politics of the 'private' sphere**, in particular sexuality, motherhood and bodies. Given the central importance granted the category of sex in this revolutionary politics it is not surprisingly to find a particular concern with **control over women's bodies**. One example of such an emphasis may be found in the work of Robyn Rowland and her stringent critique of new reproductive technologies like IVF (*in vitro* fertilisation).[24] Radical feminism usually deals with ideas, attitudes or psychological patterns and cultural values rather than with the economics of male domination,[25] and the (sexed) body is often the only concretely 'material' element in the analysis.

'Material', as noted earlier in this section, is a terminology that refers to concrete structural, including economic and technological, and bodily or physical aspects of social organisation. Radical feminism's relative disinterest in 'material' social issues such as waged work was, and is, often the subject of rebuke by liberal and Marxist/socialist feminists. However, radical feminists in many ways pioneered a stress on the significance of the politics of bodily materiality within feminist thought which is now well accepted within most feminist approaches. Their focus on the body as a critical site of oppression for women but also as representing women's difference and therefore to be celebrated, stands in sharp contrast to liberal feminism's general aim of reducing or preferably eradicating attention to bodies and bodily difference as politically retrograde.[26]

Radical and Marxist/socialist feminists have more in common here in the sense of acknowledging that social life is embodied but, as will shortly become evident, the inclination of the latter feminist approach is frequently to limit interest in embodiment to the labouring body of the paid (or less often, the unpaid) worker and more specifically to investigation of the sexually differentiated activities and jobs undertaken by women waged workers. Radical feminists tend to leave workforce activities to one side but are far less unidimensional regarding the body, ranging over sexuality, sexual violence, the (maternal) reproductive body, the feminine body as a source for creativity and spirituality, and the meaning of an embodied self (feminine subjectivity and identity). Indeed, unlike Marxist/socialist feminism, radical feminism conceives **the body—and, in particular, the sexually specific body—as critical to social analysis**. Sexual difference (evident in, for example, women's capacity to give birth) is not socially insignificant nor something that will become irrelevant once old-fashioned prejudices restricting women's opportunities are abandoned.

Rather than perceiving the (sexed) body as mere, inanimate 'meat' separate from social practices, power relations or social change, this form of feminism stresses the interconnection between bodies and society. The agenda of radical feminist writings is to counter women's supposedly natural, biological, inferiority and subordination within patriarchal society by asserting their at least equal (or superior) status in relation to men: a crucial aspect of that agenda is for women to **gain control over their own bodies/biology** and relatedly to **value and celebrate women's bodies**.[27] Many aspects of radical feminism's emphasis on body politics have been taken up with enthusiasm by emerging groupings of feminists, such as psychoanalytic and postmodern/poststructuralist feminists. In focusing on the issue of 'control' over bodies, radical feminism is inclined to distinguish the self (who might take control) from the body (the object of that control) in certain respects.[28] By comparison, the latter groupings tend to give more attention to the ways in which the self and body are indistinguishably bound up.

MARXIST/SOCIALIST FEMINISM

The third major feminist tradition is Marxist/socialist feminism. Marxist feminism was an influential school of Western feminist thought in the 1960s and 1970s. While the impact of Marxism on feminist theory remains evident in a number of contemporary approaches (such as psychoanalytic and postmodern/poststructuralist feminisms, as well as those concerned with race/ethnicity), the Marxist feminist tradition is waning. Its place in advocating the significance of Marxism/socialism and class analysis for feminism has now largely been overtaken by a range of socialist feminisms.

Indeed **Curthoys** asserts that *both* the Marxist and socialist feminist traditions 'more or less died at the end of the 1980s, when socialism itself collapsed throughout Eastern Europe'.[29] Curthoys is by no means alone in her concern that the meaningful use of terms like Marxist or socialist may have fallen out of favour within feminism[30] and that feminism may have abandoned the issues most associated with this grouping such as economics, class, historical analysis and interventions in social policy development.[31] **Cockburn**, for example, declares that 'in some countries of Europe one finds few women today who will describe themselves as socialist feminists, or even Marxist feminists'.[32] Nevertheless, the pronouncement of socialist feminism's eclipse seems a little premature. While few feminist theoreticians in the 1990s continue to describe themselves as Marxist feminists,[33] some groups of Marxist feminists continue to be politically active and are usually found within broadly based Marxist organisations or parties, rather than in specifically feminist associations.[34] Additionally, there are any number of activists and writers firmly within the socialist feminist tradition, as well as many contemporary theorists who may be regarded as being influenced by and engaged in reworking the boundaries of that tradition.

In this context, Curthoys' pessimism may be tempered by caution. She is herself an example of the ongoing existence of socialist feminist thought. Curthoys has produced a considerable body of analysis on theories concerning women and work and, in discussion with Rosemary Pringle, has articulated a classic form of the debate between socialist and postmodern feminist approaches.[35] Other writers[36] within the tradition include many (if not most) feminist writers producing work on social and public policy—particularly policy linked to the welfare state; a fair proportion of writers who produce feminist texts with a social sciences (sociology, history, law, politics) orientation or which discuss 'family' and 'work'; most of the writers in the field of feminist studies of technology, labour and economics, and much of the work in the field of feminist analyses of masculinities. The variety of writers who are influenced by but concerned with reformulating and transforming the socialist feminist agenda ranges from feminists dealing with racism to those who are more or less interested in intersections with postmodernism.[37] Nevertheless, it should be noted that socialist thought has historically been more influential in Europe, Britain and countries like Australia than in North America, and for this reason it continues to have a differential significance in different cultures within Western feminism.[38]

In order to understand the impact of socialism in feminist thought it is necessary to consider first the approach taken in Marxist feminism, since it was this form (rather than pre-Marxian 'Utopian' socialism) which became the subject of revived feminist interest in the twentieth century.[39] In **Marxist feminism**, following the work of Karl Marx,[40] hierarchical class relations (built on unequally distributed or owned sources of wealth, including monetary and other resources) are seen as *the* source of coercive power and oppression, of all inequalities ultimately. **Sexual oppression is seen as a dimension of class power**. In this model the earliest forms of class division historically gave rise to male dominance; class oppression predates sex oppression. The emerging organisation of the first forms of private wealth, and therefore of class hierarchy, led to the treatment of women as property. In other words Marxist feminism offers a version of history and society which is in some ways the opposite of that proposed by radical feminism. (In radical feminism the earliest forms of male domination over women produce a framework of hierarchical social relations in which class divisions arise; sexual oppression predates class power.) Clearly what is at stake in this difference of views is the question of which is the primary oppression for women, and hence which should be given the highest priority in feminist political struggle.[41]

By comparison with radical feminism there is typically less concern within Marxist feminism with ideas and attitudes and more of a focus on labour and economics when exploring women's positioning. Since **labour** is viewed as fundamental to all economic activity, (historically specific) analysis of the organisation of labour is crucial to Marxist feminist approaches. Indeed, the **organisation of labour** and the **tools/technologies** associated with labour are perceived in concert as constituting the underlying economic structure or system of society. This economic structure conditions the form of all other social relations in that society and in this sense is the *basis* of society.[?] Hence Marxist feminists, in common with other Marxists, generally accept some version of what is called the **base–superstructure** model of society, that is, social relations— including those related to sexual inequality—are conceived as crucially shaped by the **economic base** of society, rather than by ideas and attitudes.

The Marxist feminist approach tends, like liberal feminism, to be oriented towards the public sphere and, given its concern with the organisation of labour, generally pays particular attention to women's position in relation to **waged labour**. The significance of unpaid labour undertaken in the private realm, which is very much associated with women, is controversial in Marxist feminism because Marxism largely equates 'the economy' with the capitalist market-place.[43] However, unlike liberal feminists, Marxist feminist thinkers are deeply antagonistic to the capitalist economy and advocate a **revolutionary** approach in which the **overthrow of capitalism** is viewed as *the* necessary precondition to dismantling male privilege.[44]

Relatedly, there is less emphasis in this model than in radical feminism upon men's involvement in power or the benefits for men of unequal power relations. Power is not primarily associated with sex but with the imperatives of class, private wealth, property and profit. One example of this inclination to describe women's subordination within the terms of a Marxist account of the requirements of class society may be found in the work of Lise **Vogel**.[45]

The 'main enemy' in this form of analysis is the class system (capitalism, in modern societies) which creates divisions between men and women. Marxist feminism shares with liberal feminism (both are what Grosz has described as 'equality' or 'egalitarian' feminisms), an assumption that there is an underlying **sameness** between men and women.[46] While women seem to be oppressed by the men around them, they—like men—are ultimately oppressed by capitalism, and hence the 'interests' of men and women are not crucially different.[47]

SOCIALIST FEMINISM

Debates between radical feminists and Marxist feminists in the 1960s and 1970s concerning the fundamental cause of social inequality were important in the formation of new groupings of socialist feminism.[48] Socialist feminists attempt to maintain some elements of Marxism regarding the significance of class distinctions and labour while incorporating the radical feminist view that sexual oppression is not historically a consequence of class division. In other words all socialist feminists assert, along with radical feminists, that women's subordination pre-dated the development of class-based societies and hence that women's oppression could not be *caused* by class division. There are several versions of socialist feminism which involve **different combinations of radical and Marxist feminism**, and which sometimes incorporate the influence of psychoanalytic feminisms.[49]

In brief, three major socialist feminist traditions may be described as deriving from debates between radical and Marxist feminists. The first strand involves a concern with the social construction of sex (gender) which was largely seen in terms of Freudian psychoanalysis. This approach tends not to perceive sexual oppression through the lens of women's unequal socio-economic position—in Marxist terms the so-called 'material' organisation of social life—but rather conceives that oppression as the effect of psychological functions. At the same time the approach continues to make use of a Marxian understanding of class relations. Hence this first strand of socialist feminism offers what has been termed a **dual systems** model of social analysis, investigating **sex** and **class** power according to differ-ent procedures and identifying two 'systems' of social organisation corresponding to these forms of power, that is, **patriarchy** and **capitalism**. In broad terms a psychological model of sexual power is presented alongside an (historically specific) economically based account of class power. Moreover, the former is moulded or historically contextualised by the organising force of the latter. Because the overall model makes use of Marxist 'materialism' (that is, a methodology which sees economics as the fundamental motor of social relations—shaping the form of society), it tends to adopt a version of the Marxist base–superstructure model in which class is still ultimately fundamental (base) since sex is (merely) psychological (superstructure). Hence, in some ways this is more a **two-tier**, rather than a mutual or dual, theory of social relations. The two-tier approach is epitomised by the early work of Juliet Mitchell.[50]

The second major strand of socialist feminism attempts to draw the work of radical and Marxist feminists into one theory of power and describes a **unified system** sometimes referred to as **capitalist patriarchy** (although this term is also used by other feminists, including other socialist feminists). Examples of this approach include work by Alison Jaggar and Iris **Young**.[51] By contrast, the third strand—like the first— describes a 'dual system' model of social organisation. However, in this case both sex and class power have a **material** aspect, that is, they both are conceived as having an economic form. In other words, **patriarchy is not seen as simply psychological**, as is the case in the first variant associated with Juliet **Mitchell**. The third form of socialist feminism offers a more full-blown account of both systems in which sexual and class oppression interact but are not cast as dependent forms. Neither is viewed as more fundamental than the other in the overall shaping of social relations. The work of Heidi **Hartmann** provides the classic example of this 'dynamic duo' approach.[52]

These versions of socialist feminism are identified by their views of the relationship between class and sex (sometimes referred to as the category, gender)—that is, the relationship between capitalism and patriarchy. Other categories of power such as race tended to be marginalised in initial accounts of debates among socialist feminists. Indeed the issue of race and/or ethnicity, for example, increasingly became a point of contention within socialist feminism given its concern with forms of power that cut across both class division and sexual difference.[53] Recently, such debates have contributed to the development of certain 'postcolonial' feminist perspectives, indicating ongoing interactions between socialist feminist themes and feminist concerns regarding race/ethnicity. I will return to this point in chapter 8.

6

'Other' possibilities: feminism and the influence of psychoanalysis

By the 1980s Western feminism could no longer be simply divided up into the three general categories of liberal, radical and Marxist/socialist traditions. Many other approaches, drawing upon an increasingly eclectic and sometimes rather inaccessible range of social and political theories, became a feature of academic feminism at least. Psychoanalysis was one of the more influential streams of thought to be re-evaluated by feminists in both English speaking and non-English speaking Western countries. While in the 1970s liberal and radical feminists rejected psychoanalysis, it began to be reconsidered as an element within the work of some Marxist/socialist feminists. However, my focus in this chapter is upon those feminist viewpoints which *organise their theorising* around some form of psychoanalytic theory. Such viewpoints are diverse, and include writers such as Juliet Mitchell whose earlier work was more clearly within the Marxist/socialist feminist tradition. Despite such diversity, **psychoanalytic feminists** share—in common with radical feminism—an interest in the issue of **difference** in relation to the sexes; a concern with the notion of women as **other** than men.

In broad terms the influence of psychoanalysis has produced two major variants. The first of these is Freudian feminism which has attended to the significance of psychology and the formation of sexually specific personalities (subjectivities) in the framing of male dominance by analysing the impact of women's responsibility for mothering. Freudian feminism is

65

associated with certain English speaking, particularly North American, writers.[1] The second grouping draws upon the work of Jacques **Lacan**, an interpreter of Freud's analytic method, who stresses the fraught fragility of sexual identity and its links to language acquisition. Lacanian feminist approaches are usually linked with French and to a lesser extent some British and Australian writers.[2] Two sub-groups within Lacanian feminism may be distinguished—that is, those who more or less follow Lacan's interpretation of psychoanalysis and those who may be described as 'post' Lacanians (otherwise known as 'French feminists' or the 'écriture feminine' school). The following chapter is restricted, for the sake of brevity, to a description of the frameworks of Freudian and post-Lacanian feminists, with only passing reference to views which show more commitment to Lacanian analysis. The links between post-Lacanian and 'corporeal' feminists who focus on the body are also briefly outlined.

FREUDIAN FEMINISTS

Misgivings regarding the significance that Marxism attached to economics, which were evident in the flowering of socialist feminist thought in the 1960s, also produced other forms of feminist work. Many Western feminists by the 1970s considered that the radical Left focused on too narrow a conception of power. In giving priority to the economic structure of capitalism the Left were thought to have underestimated crucial processes relevant to sexual oppression such as the **formation of (sexed) identities** (masculinity and femininity). In this context, as Marxism was reassessed, some feminists welcomed a growing interest in psychological, not just economic, aspects of power. This produced a range of new feminist perspectives.

In the United States in particular a grouping of **Freudian feminists** emerged who paid special attention to the **impact of women's primary care-giving responsibilities on personality and social relations**. The fact that in all societies it is women who primarily parent/nurture children is taken to be of great relevance to social and political theory in this approach. These psychoanalytic feminists draw on the work of Sigmund **Freud** in their discussions of how it is that women become feminine and thus come to mother, but also offer a re-interpretation of his account of how the (sexed) self is formed. Freud stresses the significance of 'the Father' in shaping psychic (unconscious) life. The Father is understood here as a generalised cultural symbol of male authority partially recognisable in specific fathers/men—that is, recognisable in those marked as possessing penises. However, Freudian feminists are inclined to stress the **prior (pre-linguistic) importance of the Mother**.

Such a viewpoint clearly involves a critical reassessment of Freud and his focus on a male ordering principle in the formation of the self. Relatedly, it also involves a **re-evaluation of Freud's account of femininity**. Freud saw femininity as being formed out of envious longing for (the attributes of) the Father, which he termed 'penis envy'.[3] Emphasis on the prior impact of the Mother in Freudian psychoanalytic feminist writings results in a more positive conception of feminine sexual identity, somewhat reminiscent of themes in radical feminism. Hence, by contrast with Freud's approach, in Freudian feminist writings the psychological and cultural influence of women in the constitution of subjectivities and social relations is largely viewed as active and positive, despite their oppressed status. Instead of conceiving women as unconsciously shaped by envy for what appears to belong exclusively to men, and in relation to a male standard against which they *must* appear deficient, women are regarded as positively contributing an alternative psychological order. Accordingly, women are viewed as having much to offer to a programme for political change and indeed the exemplar of Freudian feminism, Nancy **Chodorow**, effectively suggests that the feminist political agenda should be directed towards feminising men.[4]

On this score, Chodorow's form of 'difference feminism' may be usefully compared with the 'equality feminism' of liberal feminists. Though both Chodorow and liberal feminists argue that men and women ought to become more alike, the latter emphasise women's capacity to take on many of the activities or qualites associated with men, while Chodorow stresses the advantages of men becoming more like women in terms of developing nurturing, empathetic characteristics. Chodorow argues in this context that shared child-rearing would have a dramatic effect on the organisation of sexual oppression by undermining the current constitution of masculinity, a masculinity presently built upon disconnection from and power over others.

Chodorow, in common with other writers in this grouping like Carol **Gilligan** and Sara **Ruddick**, offers an emphasis on and celebration of 'women's fundamentally different sense of self',[5] a 'unique female voice'.[6] Gilligan describes a different form of moral reasoning employed by women and Ruddick refers to 'maternal thinking'. Both writers challenge mainstream Freudian notions of woman being deficient. For Chodorow difference between the sexes is formed out of inequitable social arrangements—women's unequal responsibility for nurturing—and yet is seen as offering possibilities for a better world. Sexual difference, though intimately linked with oppression, is positively affirmed in a re-interpretation of women's qualities which challenges the use of a male standard for all. Ironically, that which has marked women as deficient in a male dominated sexual hierarchy becomes both a means to reject women's devaluation and a source of hope for the future.

In Freudian feminism, change in existing social arrangements is crucially a matter of intervening in psychological development. Consequently, this approach has sometimes been accused of ignoring the social context in which sexually differentiated characteristics or experience arise.[7] This charge has arisen despite elements of socialist thought (which is typically concerned with 'the social') within the work of some writers in this grouping. For example, **Chodorow** takes from strand three of socialist feminism a **dual system** approach and hence sees women's position as at least linked to both class and sex (capitalism and patriarchy). However—like Juliet Mitchell's version of socialist feminism (strand one) and many radical feminist writers—in practice Chodorow pays little attention to class or race and perceives sex largely in terms of inner psychological processes, that is, in terms of the unconscious (the psyche), sexual identity and personality. In other words, she **focuses on the category of sex (on patriarchy)** and within this tends to depict the **sexual system as a matter of psychology**, despite some references to economic processes such as the sexual division of labour within that system.[8] This inclination to prioritise psychology as a crucial, sometimes almost exclusive, theme is characteristic of the work of Freudian feminists and indeed may be argued to be even more evident in Lacanian feminist thought.

LACANIAN FEMINISTS

The interplay of Marxist/socialist and radical feminist thinking with psychoanalysis produced a specific mode of Freudian feminism largely developed in the USA which **links unconscious mental phenomena** (sexed subjectivities)—and specifically the unconscious construction of femininity as a nurturing, maternal or 'relational' personality—with **concrete macrosocial relations between men and women**. This linkage is noted with the aim of developing **tangible sociopolitical strategies** out of an understanding of the importance of intangible psychological structures.

A similar mix of influences (Marxism/socialism, radical feminism and psychoanalysis) has also produced rather different kinds of psychoanalytic feminist thought. This is particularly evident in France. Indeed feminist writers in France from the 1960s onwards generally indicate a familiarity with both Marxism and psychoanalysis that is much less common among feminists from English-speaking countries. Nevertheless, some writers in the English-speaking world (such as Juliet **Mitchell** and Jacqueline **Rose**), along with certain French feminists (including writers like Luce **Irigaray**, Hélène **Cixous** and Julia **Kristeva**), have concentrated upon a reworking of Freudian psychoanalysis which employs the approach of French psychoanalyst, Jacques Lacan.

This beginning point is at a distance from the comparatively more social (sociological) framework and concerns of the Freudian-based North American variety of psychoanalytic feminism insofar as Lacan's writings describe the development of the (sexed) self in linguistic or symbolic-cultural terms rather than in the more concrete, literal, even biological terms, sometimes favoured by Freud. For example, in Lacan's work 'penis envy' is no longer seen as involving envy of the literal biological organ as it is in Freud's thinking, but has a thoroughly symbolic–cultural meaning, rather more along the lines of a psychological positioning as 'lacking' in relation to the authority/power associated with the masculine.

In this context, Lacan refers to 'the phallus' rather than to the penis. The phallus is not so much a thing (though it may be represented by the penis or father) as the symbol of that which is not-the-mother. While the child initially does not distinguish its self as distinct and exists in a symbiotic relationship with the mother, the phallus provides the means by which the child learns that all is not one and the same, that distinctions can be made. In other words, the phallus enables the child to discover sexual difference, and its (sexual) positioning in relation to that difference. The phallus, therefore, breaks up (penetrates) the seamless interconnecting world of mother–child, alerting the child to the meaning of difference *per se*. And, because for Lacan language, culture and meaning itself are organised as a symbolic system of differences, he describes the phallus as the ultimate signifying mechanism.[9] Since it provides the key by which the child encounters difference, the phallus enables the child's entry into culture and society by the development of a self (an 'I' recognised as being distinct or different from others). All children thus become 'subjects' (develop a self) through the operation of a masculine regulatory principle. According to Lacan, 'civilisation' itself *is* the 'Law of the Father'.

The influence of Lacan in the perspectives of feminists mentioned above marks a **move away from 'the real world'** towards comparatively abstract philosophical analysis of culture and specifically towards the **symbolic–cultural meaning encoded in language** (it can therefore be described as an anti-realist approach).[10] In this context language is the necessary first step by which the child enters culture but is also viewed as a sign system which organises or shapes culture by directing what can be known and recognised and what cannot: language is conceived as the foundation of, or as encapsulating, culture. Moreover, in Lacanian thought, the self and sexuality are socially constructed in that there can be no (sexed) self— no masculine or feminine person—prior to the formation of the subject in language.[11] Both society and the socially produced, sexually specified people which make up society are dependent on language which, as noted above, is conceived as being organised around a masculine standard.

FRENCH FEMINISTS (THE 'ÉCRITURE FEMININE' SCHOOL)

Given the significance accorded language within Lacan's work, it is not surprising that one of the two subgroups of feminist writers influenced by that work are sometimes depicted in terms of their concern with language. A particular strand of French Lacanian feminists are described as engaged in the project of **'écriture feminine'**, as attempting embodied feminine writing, or writing from the position of woman (from the position of the female body) in a manner that challenges the way in which woman is construed in language/culture. While this subgrouping of Lacanian feminists are most commonly labelled simply **French feminists** in the English speaking world—which rather ignores the host of other kinds of feminist traditions in France[12]—the nomenclature 'écriture feminine' is a better indicator of what is particular to this form of feminist thought. (I will make use of both trademarks.)

Whereas Lacan, in common with Freud, depicts femininity as a castrated state—as lacking or deficient by comparison with the masculine—these French feminists start from but provide a critique of this negative assessment.[13] Their more critical engagement with Lacan marks their position as rather more **post-Lacanian** than the work of writers such as Juliet **Mitchell**. While they accept Lacan's account of language/culture as a masculine order, unlike Mitchell, they do not accept his positive affirmation of that masculine order as equivalent to civilisation or sociality in releasing the child from the stagnant primitivism of its prior symbiotic link with the feminine (Mother). These post-Lacanians—in common with the approach of Freudian feminists—reject any endorsement of masculine dominance and are sceptical regarding Lacan's view that the basis of a viable self and of culture lies in refusing attachment, in disconnection from others, and in the rejection of the Mother (women). Relatedly, the school of 'écriture feminine' questions the assumption that femininity can only be seen from the point of view of phallic culture (culture as masculine dominance) and argues for other possibilities.[14]

In order to understand this approach some further comments on the work of Lacan may be helpful. For Lacan each person becomes a person, enters human culture, by internalising society's communicative rules or **Symbolic Order**. This occurs through the formation of a separate and sexually specific (unconscious) self in the process of learning language. Individuals can only speak in the tongue of the Symbolic Order but that order is viewed in psychoanalytic terms as the **Law of the Father**. In Lacanian thought, following Freud, culture *is* masculine, not just presently male dominated.[15] Femininity is no more than the negative pole in relation to the symbolic rules which regulate individuals and hence society. Femininity is unspeakable except in the terms of masculinity: there is no feminine outside the phallic order of language.[16] The project of 'écriture feminine' accepts the Lacanian account of femininity's outsider status but proposes developing an alternative language, a way of thinking, which might make use of that status. **The feminine** is therefore not merely construed as **lack**, from which nothing can be generated, but as offering a **rebellious cultural creativity**.[17]

In this context French feminists take from the existentialist writings of Simone de Beauvoir the notion of woman as the second sex or 'Other', but, unlike de Beauvoir, perceive the invisibility/marginality associated with the feminine as representing an opportune positioning for critical assessment of what is valued and legitimated in the Symbolic Order.[18] Hence they are distinguished by rejecting the cultural assumption that women can only be seen in (the) terms of men and by a form of writing which claims the possibilities of femininity. Though radical feminism may be seen as initiating this manoeuvre, unlike most radical feminist work French feminist approaches **refuse to specify the content of femininity**, viewing such specification as a repetition of patriarchal imperatives which continually tell us what women are and must be.[19]

For the 'écriture feminine' writers, the notion of 'Woman' exemplifies the cultural and linguistic principle of rendering inferior that which does not fit *the* (masculine) norm and refusing to acknowledge or value difference from the norm— that is, refusing to recognise difference of any kind, not just sexual difference. Woman demonstrates the operation of hierarchical differentiation within phallic culture rather than bearing a set content. Thus femininity is celebrated as offering the potential for interrogation of the singular yardstick of the Symbolic Order (the Rule of the Father): in other words, femininity offers a possible procedure for subverting the marginalising mechanisms of power, thereby breaking it up.

This stress on the positive benefits of the feminine as 'other' as a means of questioning that which is socially privileged, combined with an insistence on the indeterminacy of the feminine (the marginalised), draws on the **poststructuralist** thinking of Jacques **Derrida**. Derrida proposes that meaning in the Symbolic Order is not inevitable or intrinsic but is constantly being culturally and linguistically *produced* through a process of hierarchical differentiation, a setting up of differences characteristically organised in oppositional pairs (man/woman) with one term within each pair designated as superior or positive. 'Man', for instance, is constituted as not-woman. The concept is shaped out of the invisible exclusion of the feminine 'Other' and is utterly dependent on that hierarchical relationship. Thus Derrida describes our very conceptual apparatus, how we can think, as saturated with power and marked by the non-recognition of that power such that hierarchy appears as unremarkable.[20]

In this setting Derrida directs our attention to the *constructed* nature of hierarchical dualisms which constitute the Symbolic Order, and demonstrates that hierarchies of meaning (forms of power) in culture are neither natural nor eternal by indicating the unacknowledged dependence of that which is culturally privileged on that which is repressed. Hence he is concerned with the **deconstruction** or unpacking of the cultural/linguistic assumptions regarding the fixity and inevitability of forms of power with the aim of opening up alternative possibilities.[21] By focusing on the *significance* of that which has been **marginalised**, strategically **reversing the usual conceptual order**, Derrida develops a critical tactic for French feminists like **Irigaray**.[22] As far as these feminists are concerned, woman, as *the* exemplary embodiment of the repressed 'Other', is not a fixed essence so much as a device to invert and hence destabilise the existing conceptual order (the Symbolic Order which is patriarchal).

FRENCH FEMINISM AND INTERSECTIONS BETWEEN MODERNISM AND POSTMODERNISM

The 'écriture feminine' school may be located at the **intersection** of feminist frameworks which were either refined (liberal, Marxist, socialist) or emerged (radical) in the 1960s and 1970s and those termed **postmodernist/poststructuralist** which became more prevalent (especially in the English speaking world) during the 1980s and 1990s.[23] As a result, this grouping of French theorists provides a useful way of broadly demonstrating how postmodernist/poststructuralist feminist approaches might be *initially* distinguished from all the forms of feminism so far outlined. For example, the stress on language and meaning in the work of these French feminists is indicative of postmodernist/poststructuralist elements in their analyses.

Many varieties of feminism prior to the development of postmodernism/poststructuralism recognised the significance of language and have noted that it does not simply express but also *constructs* meaning in a male dominated culture.[24] (Think of the different connotations of 'spinster' versus 'bachelor' in this context!) However, French feminists focus on language-meaning in a manner which is characteristic of the postmodern/poststructuralist inclination to move away from supposedly direct considerations of 'the real world' (in the sense of simple observation of the tangible matter of physical things and social structures—such as the organisation of domestic labour) towards the study of how meaning is constituted in a culture (forms of representation). This emphasis on **meaning over matter**[25] is not a rejection of the existence of 'reality' but rather reflective of a postmodern/poststructuralist perspective that 'reality' cannot be grasped in some direct way free of social values.[26] Since in this perspective 'the real world' (including the body) can only be known in the terms or language of one's culture—there is no value-free perspective— it is not surprising that the school of 'écriture féminine' places such importance on the project of deconstructing and subverting language.

On the other hand this kind of 'French feminism' may also be perceived as retaining certain features in their approaches which are rather like those found in earlier (modernist) feminist frameworks To the extent that feminists associated with the project of 'écriture féminine' draw on (Lacanian) psychoanalysis they provide a perspective that in some respects is not straightforwardly located as postmodern/poststructuralist. In order to explain this point a very brief comparison of the terms, 'modern' and 'postmodern' is necessary. This comparison will be extended in chapter 7.

A distinguishing aspect of what has been described as **modernist** thought is **the impulse towards large-scale explanatory claims**. Society is typically said to be **structured** by some **underlying foundation** and power, oppression and hierarchy within society may thus be understood by revealing the nature of this **causal inner truth**. So-called modernist thought is therefore characteristically inclined to depict sociopolitical analysis as rather like a detective story: society is a mystery which can be unravelled by methodical interpretation of surface clues until its concealed truth is unmasked, a truth (or essence) which will explain everything. Within liberalism this theoretical core may be found in a conception of the nature of human beings as rational (self-interested) competitive individuals, while in Marxism the basis of society is located in the economic infrastructure. Such **universalised accounts** attempt to provide an all-encompassing explanation for human history and social relations. Postmodern/poststructuralist thinking, while drawing on modernism, supposedly comes after and goes beyond this kind of theoretical enterprise, reacting to it and dismantling its pretensions. (Such thinking is therefore not inevitably or straightforwardly *anti*-modernist.)[27]

The French feminists' somewhat ambivalent location in relation to postmodern/poststructuralist theory is connected to their investment in psychoanalysis, a mode of thought which presents the constitution of the unconscious as a product of the underlying order or structure of the Law of the Father. In classical Freudian psychoanalysis (sexed) subjectivity created within a masculine code is presumed to be a universal feature of human culture, while the Law of the Father is situated as the founding truth of that culture. Psychoanalysis in this sense is a paradigmatically modernist mode of thought.[28] While Irigaray, for example, refutes the psychoanalytic view that male dominance (the Law of the Father) is necessary to culture and hence inevitable, she does accept its status as the inner core of sociality thus far and the irreducible sexual difference it prescribes.[29] The universal explanatory claims and exclusion of other forms of explanation that mark classical psychoanalysis remain evident in the work of writers of the 'écriture feminine' school. The work of Freudian feminists more clearly indicates a debt to modernist thinking, but both Lacanian and post-Lacanian feminist writings also share certain features of that mode of thought.

Customary conceptions of 'modern' and 'postmodern' thinking revolve around depicting the latter as offering a challenge to the former—that is, depicting some distinction between the two which should inhibit, at least, their coexistence within the same framework. The French feminists unsettle such conceptions because they apparently employ aspects of both. This suggests that postmodern/poststructuralist theories may well be more similar to and more reliant on modernist–structuralist ideas, and/or that the latter always contained more uncertainties proclaimed to be the province of the former, than polemical debates in feminism and elsewhere sometimes assert. Nevertheless, comparison of modernism/structuralism and postmodernism/poststructuralism does enable some broad clarification of the ways in which they are usually distinguished.

Such a comparison is useful when exploring the characteristics of different strands of psychoanalytic feminist thought (and, in the following chapter, the characteristics of postmodern/ poststructuralist feminist perspectives).

FRENCH FEMINISM, CORPOREAL FEMINISM AND THE BODY

Having briefly summarised the work of post-Lacanian feminists and their positioning in relation to poststructuralism/ postmodernism, one off-shoot or interpretation of the work of this grouping—particularly of Luce Irigaray's writings— requires specific mention. A loose collection of contemporary thinkers employing 'French' feminist thought, with its combination of psychoanalytic/Lacanian and poststructuralist/ Derridean influences, has been significant in developing feminist theories of 'the body' and the body's significance in social analysis.

This collection of thinkers—associated with Australian philosophers Elizabeth **Grosz** and Moira **Gatens**, among others[30]—proposes a **corporeal feminism** suggesting that the body can be understood as the **primary site of the embodied and sexually differentiated social practices** which produce social life and, relatedly, as **constituting the form and lived experience of the (embodied/sexed) self**.[31] In this setting the focus for long-standing feminist discussions concerning the sexualised character of social hierarchy shifts away from its stress on 'externalised' imposition—the oppression of women through socialisation in sexual 'roles' and sexual division in the workplace—typically associated with liberal, Marxist/socialist and, to some extent, radical feminisms. Corporeal feminists move towards a more intimate and physical ('internalised') politics conceived in terms of the formation of our socially produced bodies–selves.

Such writers are by no means alone in articulating an interest in the body. The recent prominence of a focus on the body across a range of contemporary feminist writings draws upon a legacy of feminist arguments. They include arguments around biopolitical issues such as reproduction, sexuality and sexed/bodily subjectivity mostly associated with radical feminism. Additionally, feminists have offered critiques of mainstream thought's antagonism to the body (and its preference for the supposed superiority of the mind). Such critiques link this antagonism with patriarchal conceptions of women as being closer to unthinking Nature/biology. However, current interest in rethinking ideas of the body as simply static biology separate from social influences and questioning the presumed centrality of the conscious or rational mind, has also derived from two further reference points employed by contemporary feminists. These reference points are found in psychoanalysis from Freud onwards, with its stress on the unconscious and embodied character of social practices and subjectivity, and in the work of poststructuralist, Michel **Foucault**, who emphasises the sociohistorical, rather than natural, construction of bodily selves.

Corporeal feminists make use of many of these threads in developing a particular interpretation of French feminism. In keeping with both radical feminism and the psychoanalytic framework of the 'écriture feminine' school, corporeal feminists assume that the formation of the body–self, of subjectivity, occurs through the child's internalisation of sexual differentiation. In other words, the latter grouping accepts the psychoanalytic dictum that there is no (social) self without sexual difference: there is no sexually undifferentiated being in social life. No disembodied asexual notion of mind or reason can then be proposed as the foundation of *human* (singular, species-based) nature and, importantly, any universalised or singular human qualities are questioned because there is **not just one form of body–self, but at least two**.[32] This insight regarding the diversity of bodily experience is taken as informing any understanding of social life. Corporeal feminists argue, therefore, that an embodied social analysis cannot assume universality or sameness among human beings. Hence, liberal feminist concepts like the 'equality' of men and women and (desexualised) 'individual' rights come under scrutiny.[33]

Corporeal feminists also follow the psychoanalytic perspective of the 'écriture feminine' school in their concern with feminine writing (writing from the position of the female body) as a means of highlighting the significance of sexually specific bodies–selves. However, insistence in psychoanalysis that paradigmatic priority be given to social differentiation and hierarchy on the basis of sex—to 'the constituting role of sexual difference'[34] in shaping the self and society—may be somewhat moderated by the cautious use of Foucault within some corporeal feminist work. The feminine writing of French feminists strategically asserts the positive aspects of the feminine—the marginalised 'Other'—while giving no particular content to the feminine. By comparison, Foucault's approach challenges the notion of specific sexual identities—no matter how indeterminate their content—and hence questions their significance, let alone priority, in the constitution of society (see chapter 7).[35]

The extent to which corporeal feminists employ Foucauldian themes may indicate a version or reworking of 'French feminism', since such themes are likely to unsettle the authority of psychoanalysis as a theory which outlines the primary significance of sexual difference. On the other hand, corporeal feminists do not straightforwardly adopt Foucault's poststructuralist stance on precisely the grounds that he typically discusses the body as a sexually undifferentiated category and therefore does not sufficiently recognise the existence of at least two kinds of bodies (that is, sexual difference). Grosz, in this context, seems to recommend the employment of both French feminist psychoanalytic thinking and Foucauldian poststructuralism, giving neither primacy, while others remain more firmly critical of Foucault.[36]

In addition, corporeal feminist writings appear to offer a particular analysis of or even departure from French feminism in their **willingness to refer to the body's physicality**—to its concrete, anatomical and physiological presence. This is in contrast to other more textual or cultural interpreters of French feminism who perceive the body in terms of how it is culturally represented.[37] The corporeal account asserts that taking embodiment seriously involves a recognition of (sex-specific) bodily existence such that bodies cannot be simply *reduced* to a set of social or cultural values devoid of physicality any more than society can be reduced to biological imperatives. Accordingly, in such an account no aspect of the body is outside of social life and no line is drawn between biology and social practices because they are seen as inextricably intertwined: body and society are one.[38] In other words, there is some reference to the 'stuff' of bodies, the matter of 'the real world' and not only to symbolic or cultural meaning in the corporeal approach.[39]

In this sense, 'corporeal' feminism expresses a renewed interest in the problems associated with integrating the body into social analysis—linked to both the long history of the body's marginalisation and separation from the social in Western thought, and the tendency to slip into biological determinism when outlining embodied conceptions of the self and society (evident in Freud's original psychoanalytic framework). The concern with matter *and* meaning in this corporeal approach suggests a particular variation of the intersections between modernist and postmodernist thinking which have already been pointed out in relation to 'French' feminism. Certainly both French and corporeal feminist writings challenge simple notions of an opposition between modernist and postmodernist thought and, in so doing, support the possibility of eclectic choices in feminist thinking.

7

More on the menu: postmodernist/poststructuralist influences

Feminist writings influenced by postmodern/poststructuralist thinking stress **plurality** rather than unity and, in particular, reject conceptions of women as a homogeneous category. The emphasis here is upon differences both within and between subjects (not just sexual difference) and relatedly the diversity of forms of power. Sexual hierarchy is not accorded any straightforward priority. In contrast to much of feminist thought, feminists who have taken up postmodernist/ poststructuralist themes **disavow universalised and normalising accounts of women as a group** (such as, all women are either the same as men or have a unique voice) on the basis that a feminism framed by such accounts becomes itself complicit in subordination. Terms like 'universalising' and 'normalising' are employed by postmodern/poststructuralist feminists in particular to detect certain problems in feminist and other theories. In this setting, universalism may be described as an analytical procedure that can only assert similarities and refers to that which is ubiquitous, thereby establishing what is 'normal' (appropriate, good, proper, natural).[1] Postmodern/poststructuralist feminists argue that universalism marginalises what is seen as dissimilar, thus bringing into play normalisation, which declares dissimilarity abnormal and attaches a negative judgment to non-conformity.

Postmodern/poststructuralist feminists assert that universalising principles are not innocent. These are viewed as intimately connected with domination and the subordination and censorship of that which does not conform. The obvious example here is the notion of the universal human being in traditional Western thought who is presented as neutral but is actually founded in a male standard. Similarly, conceptions of women as a homogeneous group are regarded as actually installing a hegemonic female subject which censors out the historical, social and other forms of diversity both within and between women. Because postmodern/poststructuralist feminists are critical of universalising/normalising procedures, they question any assumption of a shared singular identity among women (an identity typically conceived as based in a universalised experience of oppression) and note the necessary exclusion of that which does not fit within this. Thus postmodern/poststructuralist feminists adopt a sceptical stance towards the focus on women as a group, a focus which typically characterises feminist frameworks.

In common with Lacanian feminist writers, they challenge the privileging of man over woman, but not on the basis of any particular characteristics deemed to distinguish all women (identifying women as a group), such as a distinguishable female experience.² There is nothing that is essential to the category 'women' in postmodern thought: it has no intrinsic qualities (no given content) that can be the subject of feminism. Postmodern/poststructuralist feminists concentrate upon destabilising the manifold operations of power, rather than mobilising political struggle around identities like women, gay or black. These feminists are ambivalent about any search for and celebration of a (positive) distinguishable group identity(ies).

While some varieties of feminism described in previous chapters—such as Marxist/socialist and Lacanian feminist approaches—also challenge universalised analyses of women as a group in certain ways, they either generally retain universalised elements in their perception of a unitary political agenda which downplays particularity and difference (Marxist/ socialist feminisms), or they employ, to a greater or lesser degree, a universalised psychoanalytic model of sexual differentiation and effectively concentrate upon sexual difference which is taken to 'stand in' for multiple differences (Lacanian feminists). There are a number of themes and individual writers that cross over several approaches revealing, as I noted in chapter 6, intersections between universalising modernist elements and postmodern concerns regarding differences. Nonetheless, feminists influenced by postmodernism/poststructuralism are rather more likely than their Marxist/socialist or even Lacanian counterparts (who draw on postmodern themes), to describe the operations of power in terms of particularity and multiplicity.

This antagonism to a singular conception of the operations of power and stress on differences is also a feature of feminist work focusing on race/ethnicity. However, such work is generally more inclined to attend to several, specific differences both within and between human beings (for instance, sex, class and race/ethnicity), rather than dealing with multiple differences or difference 'per se' which is characteristic of postmodern/poststructuralist feminist writings. In recent times, some feminists analysing race/ethnicity have employed elements of postmodern/poststructuralist feminist thought[3] but, in broad terms, the latter grouping is associated with a more fluid account of differences. Indeed, by comparison with all other existing feminist frameworks, postmodern/poststructuralist feminist writers (especially those associated with 'queer theory') may be viewed as being less tied or committed to established categories describing power relations and identities.

In this sense they may be said to offer the greatest challenge to feminism given the earlier account of feminists' concern with the subject of 'woman', a concern which places centre stage women as a category or group identified by sex differentiation. Postmodern/poststructuralist feminists question the notion of a given *content* for categories describing power and identities and the *number* of categories that are employed in feminist approaches, as do respectively Lacanian feminists and feminists dealing with race/ethnicity. But they do more than this. They **challenge the fixity and hence the very status of established categories like sex, class and race/ethnicity**. This places in doubt any straightforward assumption regarding the priority of such categories over other differences in social analysis, let alone the priority of one category (such as sex) over others. The subject of women as a category or group appears a more and more slippery proposition.

Too relentless a focus on multiplicity/heterogeneity[4] may seem to imply the abandonment of a *feminist* framework or at least of what has been regarded as characterising feminism thus far.[5] However, feminists concerned with postmodernism/ poststructuralism can be regarded as suggesting further possibilities. These might include a contingent feminism which does not presume, but actively recognises, particular areas of 'unity in diversity' or solidarity between women and which offers the oxymoron of a broadly inclusive 'community'/politics precisely constituted out of differences,[6] and/or a 'modest' feminism which stresses the partial character of its field of endeavour and the analytical and political limits of the notion of women as a group.[7]

FEMINISM AND POSTMODERNISM

The first difficulty to be encountered in a more detailed examination of postmodern/poststructuralist feminist frameworks is that postmodernism and poststructuralism are often interchangeably employed terms. Both signal a 'crisis of cultural authority' located primarily in the Western world.[8] More specifically they are usually linked to the failure of radical movements and radical theories in France to produce revolutionary changes in the 1960s. These terms thus suggest a rejection of both mainstream *and* established radical thought, a sense of disappointment, pessimism and distaste for certainty. While 'postmodernism' appears to have first been used by a British historian in relation to the despondency of the post Second World War era,[9] it is now connected—along with poststructuralism—with a rather indeterminate collection of thinkers who either write in French or who are French, for example Jean-François **Lyotard**, Jacques **Derrida** and Michel **Foucault**. However, opinions vary as to who should be included and who excluded.[10]

Postmodernism in particular is a portmanteau term covering a diverse field. Indeed there is **no unified central**

position (essential meaning) that can be straightforwardly designated as postmodern.[11] Rather, postmodernism can refer to an historical period, cultural climate, aesthetic, or theoretical or philosophical tendency. It can also refer to a number of different approaches (sometimes conflicting) just within the realm of theory, such as in different academic disciplines.[12] Such plurality is hardly surprising for, in so far as some shared definitional conception is able to be mobilised, postmodernism is identified with a **rejection of the notion of foundational truth or essence** in favour of a recognition that meaning/truth is not eternal or impartial but **constructed, through exclusion and repression**. Postmodernism appears difficult to pin down precisely because postmodernists are inclined to challenge the explanatory claims of approaches which employ the concept of a singular, unified meaning or cause. For instance, it challenges approaches, such as Marxism, which propose an account of society as *structured* by a *determining* principle. Ironically, any unity or common ground that can be identified in relation to the term, postmodernism, lies precisely in this antagonism to singular structural (underlying) explanation and the attraction to considering **multiple determinants**, to diversity, plurality and indeterminacy.

Relatedly, postmodernists assert a distaste for the hubris they associate with approaches concerned with 'depth'; a distaste for approaches which argue that everything may be understood as (simply) a representation of an inner truth waiting to be revealed. Postmodernists have a corresponding interest in **'surface'** or **appearances**, which are deemed worthy of analysis in themselves. This can translate into a concern with **popular** rather than high-brow culture. Postmodernist perspectives therefore offer a critical gaze at **modernism**, which is conceived as a mode of thought (or sometimes an era—that is, 'modernity') **characterised by universalising and totalising (all-encompassing/authoritarian) pretensions**. Modernism is linked with certainty and arrogance signalled by its inclination to search for a foundation to all phenomena (knowledge, society, history, biology, nature, et cetera).[13]

Postmodern feminists are inclined to connect modernist thinking with a particular conception of masculinity and hence draw attention to the **male bias** of (supposedly neutral) claims of universal truth. Claims to know the truth, they argue, are not neutral but sexually specific and linked to power. While this broad perception is well established in other feminist traditions, the postmodern critical deconstruction of all foundational thought—of analyses seeking underlying explanations or causes for macro phenomena—involves an innovation which presents a challenge to other feminist traditions.[14] Indeed, the postmodern critique of the universalised and totalising (all-embracing) claims characteristic of foundational thought raises questions about the project of feminism *per se*. After all, feminism's rejection of misogyny/sexual hierarchy and of women's marginality in mainstream Western thought, as well as the alternative politics this rejection generates (see chapter 4), typically involve an explanatory schema concerning male privilege which is supposed to be applicable on a broad scale.[15]

Feminists influenced by postmodern thinking propose that universalist assumptions must be unravelled within feminist thought as much as elsewhere. They therefore raise the issue of possible authoritarian elements within feminist thought itself to the extent that feminism may employ an overly unified, overly all-encompassing account of power and the category, women (a major focus of its agenda for change). Overly unified conceptions of power and the subjects of power within feminism are regarded as being dangerously authoritarian because they repress/exclude the possibility that oppression is not the same for all women, that women are not all the same. Accordingly, postmodern feminists assert that universalist assumptions could ironically produce in feminism a repetition of the very procedures of oppression feminism hopes to undermine. Their concern here is that making assumptions about Women as a group (regarding them as all the same) simply replaces the singular authority of Western 'Man' as the universal standard in traditional thought with another (feminine) controlling norm, against which some women are bound to be marginalised. This critical perspective within postmodern feminism does not necessarily amount to endorsing the abandonment of any explanatory claims, any form of general thinking, or any conception of collectivity in feminism, but certainly postmodern writings argue for unpacking the collection of ideas which characterises feminism in order to carefully scrutinise, render explicit and reconstruct the elements of that collection.[16]

A second feature of postmodernist frameworks arises in relation to their critique of modernist conceptions of human nature and the self. **Modernism** is regarded as being associated with a **humanist** perspective drawn from **Enlightenment thought**,[17] in which an original, specifically *human* nature is conceived as founded in reason. Relatedly, the self is understood to be a unified coherent identity or autonomous unit organised around this reasoning core. These concepts of human nature and the unified subject are universalised and become abstract, pre-given principles whatever the historical or cultural context. Postmodern thinkers question the idea of a central explanatory foundation or coherent core to human sociality, a notion which is perceived to be critical to the project of modernity, and instead focus on the **constructed fragility of subjectivity**, that is, its internal fragmentation as well as its diverse forms (non-universality).[18] This rejection of a rationalist account of human nature and consequent attention to the instability of subjectivity suggests some overlap between at least certain forms of psychoanalysis and postmodernism, but postmodernism's critique of universalism and singular causality is inclined to resist the macro explanatory model employed in psychoanalysis.

In keeping with its scepticism about there being a foundation to human sociality, postmodern feminism perceives the modernist account of the **unified (rational) subject**, which supposedly is what distinguishes a universal 'human' nature, as being, **'in practice modern European and male'**.[19] Such a modernist approach is therefore regarded as being crucially complicit in the representation of other groups of people as lesser human beings and thus postmodern feminists link this with the exercise of a sexual hierarchy. The links between the operations of power and the putative neutrality of modernist humanism are taken to exemplify the authoritarian effects of universalist thinking. On this basis postmodern feminism recommends exposing problems within 'humanistic discourses that presume an underlying commonality between all people' or groups of people, such as women.[20] This strategy amounts to a concern to destabilise, undermine or even perhaps dissolve the concept of identity, given its connections with the unitary human nature, or self promulgated by modernist humanism.

Not surprisingly, postmodern feminists regard the employment of **identity politics** within feminism (or other frameworks) with some disfavour. Identity politics 'invokes a sense of belonging . . . to an oppressed group' in some deeply embedded and complete way and may be said to locate categories (such as woman, black, lesbian) as the essence (the truth) of one's being.[21] Postmodern feminists perceive the employment of group identities in mobilising political solidarity as a dangerous exercise because, they argue, rather than bringing to light and celebrating some underlying authentic (unitary/fixed) self repressed by power, it involves the reiteration of identities which are themselves produced by the operations of power and are therefore not self-evidently emancipatory. In this context, postmodern feminists insist that resistance to male privilege does not involve taking as given what has been supposedly associated with women and thus they refuse to sanctify a persecuted feminine identity supposedly shared by all women.

Because of their concern to destabilise unitary conceptions of identity/self and their related scepticism regarding the emancipatory potential of such conceptions, some postmodern feminists urge the abandonment of any notion of identity, including sexual/gender identity.[22] But other postmodern feminists are more ambivalent. The latter assert that the use of a universalised or group identity in relation to women, or other categories, is *strategically* necessary in that it is not possible to undertake resistance to power from some theoretically pure position outside of the current conditions of power including the organisation of categories around sexual identity. However, the use of the category, woman, is still undertaken with reluctance and with a vigilant espousal of the problems associated with such usage.[23]

Such debates around the question of identity are not

necessarily indicative of insurmountable tensions within postmodern feminist analysis. Rather, **Spivak** argues that postmodern feminists may not always adopt a position of 'theoretical purity' in the sense of perceiving postmodern insights (such as its critique of universalism) as absolutes. Moreover, postmodernism itself can be seen not as a thorough-going repudiation of modernism and its humanist inclinations, so much as a means to question it.[24]

FEMINISM AND POSTSTRUCTURALISM

Poststructuralism is very commonly used simply as an alternative term to postmodernism. However the former can be linked with a somewhat more specific intellectual field than the latter. Poststructuralism announces a **debt to structuralism**—which is an approach with a relatively definite meaning. This lineage may suggest that poststructuralism shares broad features with postmodernism, but it is not equivalent to it. Accordingly, poststructuralism might be understood either as an approach which is distinguishable from postmodernism and hence having a separate status, or as a subset of postmodernism, in which case postmodernism may become the 'proper name' for a loose constellation of thinkers critical of the explanatory claims associated with modernism.[25] Whatever position is taken, it is worth noting that poststructuralism is a term which—along with 'French' feminism—was not developed by those writers in the French speaking world to whom it is usually attached but rather was 'made in America'.[26] The invention of the label, poststructuralism, at a cultural remove (its expropriation?)[27] may well have overly encouraged misleading conceptions of it as a coherent intellectual phenomenon. Certainly any such conceptions sit uneasily alongside variable usages of the term and that term's uncertain link with the similarly nebulous label, postmodernism.

In spite of these caveats, to the extent that poststructuralism describes a point of departure from structuralism, it can be viewed as bearing some broadly distinguishing features. The term, poststructuralism, suggests that the usefulness of the structuralist project—particularly associated with the work of Ferdinand de **Saussure**—is to some extent assumed, but also indicates a critical response to structuralism. In this context, certain features of structuralism require explanation. Saussure, a Swiss linguist, proposed that there is a formal foundation, or **underlying fixed structure, to language**. The broad principle of unearthing the fundamental structure of a designated theoretical problem came to be described as 'structuralism'. However, the term encompasses the work of those who have employed somewhat more specific elements of Saussure's 'structural linguistics'. In the latter instance, 'structuralism' indicates the application of Saussure's formulations concerning the structure of language to understanding systems of meaning more generally.

In Saussure's thinking, language is not simply a vehicle for expressing meaning. Rather, he argues, our understanding of the world is context and culture specific and hence linguistically organised. Meaning is formulated within language and is not somehow to be found outside the ways in which discourse operates. Furthermore, meaning (how we comprehend the world) is subject to the underlying structure of language: it arises through a system of relationships between terms. For Saussure, concepts do not predate language or exist in splendid isolation as individual autonomous entities but are a product of relationships—oppositions—within language. For example, 'white' is not an immutable idea or thing which stands alone. Instead, it gains its particular significance from our understanding of what is not-white. 'White' has meaning because it is enmeshed in a web of other concepts from which it is differentiated. In summary, Saussurean structural linguistics presumes that **systemic difference** (differentiation/opposition), the underlying structure of language, is **the precondition for meaning**. Saussure envisaged that this insight might be applied more broadly to the analysis of any number of cultural communicative systems.[28]

His approach has been very influential in the development of structuralist and poststructuralist thought. Theorists from both schools have taken up Saussure's suggestions regarding the broader use of his protocols *beyond* a strict focus on the rules of language, and both have tended to connect the **constitution of meaning through difference with power**—that is, meaning/truth is viewed as being constituted by exclusion and repression. In this setting, differentiation is not a neutral mechanism enabling meaning through the play of alternative choices but involves the performance of power. The meaning/truth of the term, 'Man', therefore arises out of an historically and culturally specific positioning in opposition to the subordinated term, 'Woman'. However, poststructuralist thinkers begin to part company with Saussure (and structuralism) in relation to his view that there is a fixed underlying structure ordering meaning.

Poststructuralists are, at minimum, inclined to destabilise this perception of a static structure and place more emphasis on the contextual fluidity and ongoing production of meaning, whether referring to language, communicative systems or other aspects of cultural and social life. This is to say that poststructuralists usually perceive meaning (conceptions of truth, the forms of power relations) as being neither entirely arbitrary—since particular meanings are socially legitimated while others are marginalised—nor absolute or eternal. Meaning is not random but also not fixed since it is constantly being produced within particular contexts. **Poststructuralists tend to stress the shifting, fragmented complexity of meaning (and relatedly of power), rather than a notion of its centralised order**.

The impact of both Saussure's views and this poststructuralist emphasis on fragmentation and decentring may be seen in the work of Jacques **Lacan**. Lacan argues that the constitution of the self may be understood in linguistic terms. If meaning, understanding, conceptualisation—that is, thought itself—is not pregiven, but a product of linguistic differentiation, it is but a short step to argue that the self is not an inherent phenomenon and that it is formed by the oppositional organisation of language. In keeping with Saussure's view that meaning arises not in relation to singular words or concepts but through a system of differentiation, the subject (the 'I') is not a singular autonomous individual but is constituted through the process by which the child acquires language, where 'I' only becomes meaningful in relation to loss or lack (that which is not–I). In Lacan's psychoanalytic framework this amounts to the loss and repression of the initial symbiotic relationship with the Mother. On the one hand, the subject is an 'I' which is organised by its relation to an 'Other' (not–I) and 'I' comes into being out of the child's separation from the Mother (out of the loss of the undifferentiated mother–child bond). It is that which is not-Mother. On the other hand, the subject, 'I', is formed out of a split between the unconscious (produced by the repression of the lost 'Other'/Mother) and consciousness. **The self is never one coherent unity.**[29]

Moreover, in drawing attention to the interaction between the system of language and the self, Lacan destabilises Saussure's notion of language as being a fixed structure which can be analysed in objective terms, that is, in terms which suggest a neutral order which is separable from the positioning of subjects.[30] Lacan's reworking of Saussurean structuralism is evident here. Meaning produced through a system of linguistic differentiation (through difference, in particular sexual difference) cannot be disconnected from power, as is manifest in the formation of selves shaped by the social and sexual hierarchy. In other words, **meaning/language is never neutral**—including the meaning given to identity/the self—rather it is **socially contextualised and constructed**. The influence of Lacan's work in feminist thought has been noted in chapter 6.

Themes like the shifting, fragmented, highly contextualised and constructed complexity of meaning, power and the self—as against universalised conceptions of centralised order—are all evident in the work of Michel **Foucault**, who is perhaps most commonly viewed as exemplifying poststructuralist thinking. Foucault, partly in reaction to the influence of Marxism's focus on (economic) 'materiality', insists on Saussure's recognition of the importance of meaning.[31] Foucault takes up Saussure's interest in systems of meaning and, as Saussure intended, applies the latter's notion of the constitution of meaning/truth through difference (exclusion) within language more broadly to groups of signs (discourses/knowledges).[32] In this way Foucault is less oriented than many poststructuralist writers towards language and texts in the strict sense and more concerned with how meaning/truth comes into play within social life generally.[33]

Foucault's work places the concept of absolute Truth in doubt and he argues that the search to reveal an underlying core meaning or cause—common to modernist (foundational) thought—is reliant upon the refusal and repression of other possibilities. In other words, insistence on only one meaning, on *the* Truth, is a strategy which enforces dominance and fixity. By contrast, Foucault asserts the plurality (though it is not unlimited) and constructed character of meaning in which truth is a performative exercise established by its links with power. For example, madness is not an absolute which exists and has always existed, unrelated to its social context, but is a concept constructed by the historical development of psychiatric knowledges which reveal its truth and hence place it precisely as a natural unchanging category.[34]

It can be seen from this instance that Foucault challenges the usual association of knowledge with the unveiling of ignorance and the capacity to regulate, delimit or overthrow power. Knowledge is characteristically presented as occupying a position separate from or outside of power enabling the Truth of power (its organising principle or cause) to be revealed. However, Foucault suggests that the investment of knowledges in power is such that the operations of power *produce* notions of the truth, whether these truths be madness, power as a monolithic unity, or sexual identity. This viewpoint also indicates the extent of Foucault's *departure* from what he sees as the characteristic difficulties of modernist accounts of power. Instead of regarding power as a property of someone's will, as organised by a unified determining principle, or as a thing which it is possible to escape from or overthrow (and which is associated only with top-down negative repression), his writings present a somewhat different picture.[35] **Power is not something that one 'has'**, neither is it lodged in any privileged group of people or locations. Rather **it 'is exercised' in actions**,[36] and is **'immanent in all social relationships'**.[37] **Power is not organised around a singular principle** (for example, an underlying cause of economic or sexual division) **but is multiple**.

Moreover, the mechanics of power have a capillary form that permeates in all directions and which, in particular, may be seen in the *constitution* of subjects:[38] '[power] seeps into the very grain of individuals, reaches right into their bodies, permeates their gestures, their posture, what they say, how they learn to live and work with other people'.[39] Power is therefore, according to Foucault, productive and not merely coercive. For example, it constructs subjectivities or identities, conceived not simply as conceptual but as embodied entities. Not surprisingly, Foucault does not consider that there is some authentic essential self which lies outside of power, waiting to be emancipated by the lifting of power's thrall.[40] Indeed resistance to power is conceived as 'an element of the functioning of power', even though it contributes to its 'perpetual disorder'.[41]

Foucault's stress on the constructed nature of embodied subjects as products of power, and his placement of resistance as internal to power, are important in explaining why some feminists have made use of Foucault's work and why other feminists have found some problems with it. Many feminists have found much of use in his concern to move beyond the study of meaning in the operation of texts into explicit analysis of social relations and in his questions regarding the connections between legitimated knowledges, notions of absolute Truth, and the exclusionary effects of power. Furthermore, his approach locates the body as an increasingly significant site for the operations of power and thus recognises that power is a feature of every aspect of social life, not simply of locations such as the state (government) or the military. There are considerable overlaps here with feminist approaches and struggles. However, while Foucault does not deny the systematic privileging of men over women, he also does not perceive that privileging as grounded in some essential sexual identity belonging to women. For many feminists a concern to see women in terms of social construction rather than eternal essence is hardly an issue, but Foucault goes further than this.

Feminists characteristically assert that all forms of meaning, all varieties of social construction, including the ways in which the body might be shaped and interpreted, are sexually specified and are not sex-neutral. By contrast, Foucault regards sexual/gender identity as 'no more than a subject position within a discourse'[42] and **does not explore the operations of power in relation to sexual specificity**, let alone the sexual particularity of bodily selves.[43] At the same time he habitually portrays and refers to men, presenting a masculine position in relation to power as if it were universal. Such a conjunction seems surreptitiously to maintain masculine authority under the traditional modernist guise of a universalising sexual neutrality. This is a standard criticism of Foucault's work even among those feminists who are sympathetic to his approach.[44]

Additionally, Foucault rejects the 'very idea of a stable, centred identity as a repressive fiction'[45] and construes **resistance to power as resistance to (or even liberation from) identity**. He thus disallows those feminist claims which involve some appeal to or celebration of a common identity, interests or experience shared by women as reiterating authoritarian procedures. This radical rejection of identity has also been associated with some elements in the work of 'French' feminists such as Julia **Kristeva**, but they have offered a positive valuation of feminine identity insofar as it is associated with a subversive decentring of the power of the masculine norm. Unlike Foucault, French feminists do not straightforwardly and wholeheartedly discard the idea of (sex differentiated, or embodied sexual) identity. Many other feminists, including some postmodern/poststructuralist feminists (as noted earlier in this chapter), are similarly inclined to regard Foucault's call to abandon (sexual) identity as premature in a context in which the feminine is marginalised as a matter of course, in which women are virtually unable to be represented 'except in relation to a masculine norm'.[46] Such feminists remain concerned that if the already marginalised feminine is not voiced as a form of resistance, its disappearance may not spell destabilisation of masculine authority so much as its reiteration. They suggest that unless we explicitly refer to the category, women, the prevailing focus on men remains uninterrupted.[47] Nevertheless some **Foucauldian feminists** have revelled in what may be regarded as the postmodern optimism of a perspective which regards the sexual self, indeed all that the self is, as 'a series of performances'.[48]

Judith Butler is an example of a feminist writer who is inclined to view Foucault's emphasis on plurality as presenting possibilities rather than as a problem.[49] Butler recommends, in common with Foucault, a disaggregation of sexual categories and their heterosexist binary organisation on the basis that the sexed body cannot be located outside of discursive frameworks: the body's sexuality and the direction of its desires are constructions within these frameworks.[50] For Butler, 'there is no gender identity behind the expressions of gender; that identity is performatively constituted by the very "expressions" that are said to be its results'.[51] Thus, by contrast with those feminists influenced by Foucauldian poststructuralism who caution against discarding assertions of the feminine as premature, Butler asserts that it is premature to *insist* 'on a stable subject of feminism, understood as a seamless category of women' since this insistence 'inevitably generates multiple refusals to accept the category'.[52]

POSTMODERNISM/POSTSTRUCTURALISM AND 'QUEER THEORY'

Butler's point regarding refusals of the seamless category of women appears very relevant when considering a particular form of contemporary theorising about sexuality—that is, **queer theory**. Butler, along with other feminist writers such as **Sedgwick** and **de Lauretis**,[53] employ a postmodern/poststructuralist and specifically Foucauldian approach to reject any notion of a centred stable identity which is somehow inherent. Such writers reject any notion of an 'essence' which is fixed either innately or in a socially embedded way. They assert an antagonism to (biological or social) **essentialism** and a corresponding **radical social constructivism** in relation to **sexuality/sexual identity** which is associated with the term, 'queer theory'. Instead of assuming that one's (sexual) identity is singular and fixed, this grouping of feminists perceive identity as more incoherent and malleable, as constructed. Their approach involves a preference for considering (sexual) identity in terms of plurality or disaggregation, in terms of identities and differences. In keeping with Foucault's perspective, they resist presumptions regarding an underlying commonality between all people (human nature) or groups of people (gay, black, women), and hence urge the abandonment of conceptions or categories of identity in favour of an emphasis on the constructedness of the self/identity. This emphasis recognises the constitution of the self by power relations but because, in Foucault's thinking, power itself is multiple and not only coercive, the constructedness that is envisaged is fluid rather than fatalistic. As Foucault puts it, '[s]exuality is something we ourselves create . . . We have to understand that with our desires, through our desires, go new forms of relationships, new forms of love, new forms of creation'.[54]

Such a perspective involves dissent from both the dominant organisation of sexual identity (associated with the privileging of masculine heterosexuality) and supposedly alternative or dissident positions identified with most feminist, gay and lesbian analyses (which are inclined to value marginalised sexual identities in positive terms). Feminists developing a 'queer theory' perspective **challenge both dominant and most dissident accounts of identity by asserting that sexual identity cannot be viewed as fixed**, either in the sense of the self or in relational/hierarchical terms which establish set binary oppositions. Fixity is generally assumed in conceptions of the sexed self (like masculine–male/feminine–female) and in notions of sexual desire (like heterosexual/homosexual) however these sexual identities might be valued.

The constructivism described by the term 'queer theory' is particularly thorough-going. It questions both essentialist frameworks and social constructionist frameworks which can lapse into essentialism in gay and lesbian/feminist analyses as much as elsewhere. The work of writers like Butler, for example, is clearly at odds with essentialist accounts of (homo)sexual identity, whether these accounts assert narrow or even expanded, pluralistic versions of that core identity. It is at odds therefore with some essentialist accounts in gay politics which paradoxically employ the label 'queer'. In this context **'queer'**

as a stand-alone label may be somewhat distinguished from, though it overlaps with, 'queer theory'. The former can simply suggest **dissent from the dominant organisation of sex/sexuality combined with** an assertion that homosexuality is not of mere specialist interest but critical to any discussion of the social. Relatedly, 'queer' proposes a critical stance towards present and past understandings of homosexuality.[55] It indicates that the current conjunction of terminologies, 'lesbian and gay', is insufficient, somehow restrictive or perhaps overly concerned with safe respectability, since at the very least the conjunction takes (distinctions between) sexual categories as given and conveniently ignores the threat to heterosexuality's borders raised by the possibilities of bisexuality and trans-sexuality. Thus, although **in its broadest usage 'queer' is used to undermine narrow or exclusive conceptions of homosexuality**, this attention to plurality and to some transgression of sexual categories does not necessarily imply a concern to destabilise or threaten the dissolution of the notion of (homo)sexual identity. Indeed, sometimes 'queer' is precisely involved in shoring up that identity.

'Queer' is, for example, linked with radical 'anti-assimilationist' elements within gay politics in the West. 'Anti-assimilationist' activists promote celebration of eclectic sexed identities and desires, a celebration which does not seek the approval of the mainstream. 'Queer' in this setting is used by some gay militants, such as those in organisations such as Queer Nation, who support 'outing' on the basis of their beliefs regarding the monolithic unity of homosexual identity.[56] While such militants embrace the stand-alone word 'queer' and its associations with flamboyant confrontation, the essentialist analysis they employ stands in sharp contrast to feminist and other approaches connected with 'queer theory'.

The rejection of essentialism characteristic of 'queer theory' is however also applied to some social constructionist frameworks on the grounds that these analyses are unwilling to discard certain essentialist elements. In this light many lesbian/feminist approaches (particularly those connected with radical feminism) are described as acknowledging the social rather than innate character of heterosexuality and the malleability of sexual desire, but are criticised for retaining essentialist elements—for instance, depicting the category, lesbian, as an inherent identity which lies outside of power and resists it.[57] The thorough-going social constructivism of 'queer theory', with its stress on the fluidity of sexuality and sexual identities, also enables a critique of both longstanding and recent debates within feminist/lesbian approaches concerning the appropriate political and cultural allegiance of lesbians (to the Gay or Women's movements) and the appropriate form of lesbian sexuality (conceived as including sadomasochistic practices or not).[58] These debates are argued to be reliant on a normalising and universalised (stable) conception of lesbian (sexual) identity and its relation to masculinity, which cannot be upheld. Queer theory thus problematises not only sexual identity but its relationship to other categories and their possible political agendas, suggesting that there are no pregiven allegiances, priorities or political projects. Such a perspective allows that those marked by multiple marginalised categories, such as Chicana lesbians, demonstrate the impossibility of maintaining the distinct integrity of the categories or of privileging one (such as lesbian) over the others on the grounds that it is inherently more fundamental.[59]

The work of writers such as Butler challenges *any* stable sexual identity or idea about sexuality, let alone any belief in that identity as the foundation of a sexual politics. Rather than perceiving an unalterable intelligibility within the self and desire, there is a recognition of elasticity. Consequently, instead of an unproblematised emphasis on 'coming out'—as bringing to light and celebrating some underlying authentic (sexed) self repressed by power—queer theory crosses boundaries by declaring that sex between lesbians and gay men is 'gay sex' and discusses the concept of 'male lesbians'.[60] It appears that the notion of a situated sexuality and/or sexual identity has been all but swept away.[61] This proliferating fluidity is precisely what is questioned by some feminists, including those sympathetic to the agenda of destabilising identity.[62]

Feminist criticisms of Foucault's work are reiterated here in doubts about the seeming sexual neutrality of proposals within 'queer theory' espousing the elasticity of sexual identities. In this context, some feminists question the extent to which sexual identities may be seen as equally open and subject to negotiation, given the differential positioning attached to femininity within the prevailing sexual hierarchy and the sexual particularity of bodies. Such criticisms evidence an inclination to particularise and limit the elasticity promoted in 'queer theory', to keep in mind the tenacity and longevity of hierarchical social organisation which reduces flexibility in differential ways depending upon social positioning. They also indicate a reluctance to dispense with a politics strategically linked—at least in the present social context—to (sexual) identity. The tensions between fluidity and on-going reference to categories (as socially embedded or fixed and as resistant to change) continue in the work of feminists attending to questions of race/ethnicity.

8

Reassessments and potentialities: feminists concerned with race/ethnicity

While contemporary Western feminist writings influenced by postmodern/poststructuralist thinking and those concerned with race and/or ethnicity are by no means self-evidently similar, they both attend to differences and resist homogenising accounts of women as a unified category. In particular, they critique universalising assumptions which perceive the condition of all women as being essentially the same and **refuse to suppress differences between women**. And since the category, women, identifies a group on the basis of sex differentiation, destabilising this category also **unsettles the unproblematic authority of laying stress on sexual difference** (on differences between men and women).[1] Postmodern/poststructuralist feminists and those dealing with race/ethnicity recognise that there are diverse forms of power and identity: they share antagonism to a singular conception of the operations of power and homogenised notions of women as a group. However, their point of connection is simultaneously marked by some divergence. While, as noted in chapter 7, some writers cross over these two 'types' of feminist approaches, a distinction can be broadly outlined which is useful in initially clarifying certain characteristics of feminist work dealing with race/ethnicity before moving to a more detailed examination.

Postmodern/poststructuralist feminist writers deconstruct universalising procedures in modes of thought by indicating that these procedures are not neutral but connected with dominance, in that a specific norm becomes the standard for all and that which does not conform to the norm is subordinated. On this basis they not only reject universalising procedures in mainstream thought, but also in 'dissident' forms of thinking (such as feminism), which typically employ normalising categories describing forms of power (such as sex, [hetero]sexuality, race), and associated subordinate identities (women, gay, black). Postmodern/poststructuralist feminists usually exemplify the implicit bias of universalising procedures in mainstream thought by noting that they are founded in a masculine standard which involves the subordination and/or censorship of the feminine. They point out the bias of normalising categories in dissident forms of thinking by generally referring to the ways in which sexuality or race/ethnicity are suppressed within the conception of women as a group. The point here is that **in postmodern/poststructuralist feminist writings the focus is on challenging the neutrality of universal principles**. Attention to any particular category or marginalised group is situated as an *instance* of this broader deconstructive focus and, in any case, such categories or groups are themselves deemed sites for deconstruction. In practice postmodern/poststructuralist feminists give significant attention to the consideration of women as an exemplary instance, even as they destabilise the category, and some pay more limited attention to issues of race/ethnicity.

By contrast, although those contemporary Western feminists specialising in questions about race/ethnicity reject universalising procedures as being associated with domination and ignoring differences, they are much less inclined (than their postmodern/poststructuralist counterparts) to interpret power as a fluid plurality or to describe a proliferation of differences. They are hence less inclined to subsume attention to a particular category, such as race/ethnicity, within a larger deconstructive agenda. Their work generally involves a comparatively strong tendency to articulate the intransigence of the operations of power and identities, and to situate certain specific differences both within and between people, rather than stressing the elastic character of such differences. Feminists dealing with race/ethnicity typically interpret diversity in relation to power and identity in a more circumspect way than feminists closely identified with postmodernism/poststructuralism. While the former dissent from singular and unifying conceptions of social life and challenge stereotypic conceptions of marginalised groups, this concern to disaggregate/destabilise does not translate into challenging the status of categories describing power relations and identities to the point of threatening their dissolution.

Feminists concerned with race/ethnicity are doubtful about the identification of women as a group to the extent that this implies an unselfconscious notion of women's commonality but, in particular, are often unwilling—like Marxist/socialist feminists among others—to jettison a celebration of (positive) distinguishable group identity(ies) forged in the face of marginalisation, at least in relation to race/ethnicity.[2] In practice, feminists attending to race/ethnicity largely focus on the interplay between the specific categories of sex and race/ethnicity. The location for such a focus is usually found in those positioned as marginal in both, that is, black and ethnic minority women. It is often linked with an, at least, strategic priority attached to race/ethnicity intended to counter notions of women as a homogeneous group which is taken for granted in much of feminist thought. Feminists dealing with race/ethnicity also deal, to a lesser extent, with class and sexuality in relation to that location.

BROAD FEATURES AND ISSUES

This chapter refers to contemporary (post-1970s) feminist work in the West which *concentrates* on race/ethnicity and its relation to sexual hierarchy and not to those feminist writings which mention race/ethnicity in passing. At first glance it is evident that feminist analyses dealing with the question of race/ethnicity express widely variant viewpoints. They range from those writers who problematise the claims of the category, women, but articulate considerable investment in marginalised identities related to race/ethnicity, to those who are influenced by postmodern/poststructuralist themes and suggest a somewhat more fluid, less categorical account of differences. Relatedly, the field of feminist work which concentrates upon race/ethnicity does not follow any one theoretical framework or theoretician in the sense that all the previous forms of feminism are inclined to do and, consequently, particular feminists within it may draw on feminist and other accounts of postmodern/poststructuralist, psychoanalytic or Marxist/socialist thought, as well as on writings which attend to racism/ethnocentrism.[3] (Both liberalism/liberal feminism and radical feminism are markedly less common sources.)

Given this diverse range of views and frameworks, the only assertion that is consistently reiterated within the field is **the critique of feminism** as, at minimum, **inattentive to race and ethnicity**. More often feminism is seen as being exclusionary and (either implicitly or explicitly) racist/ethnocentrist. Contemporary Western feminists focusing upon race/ethnicity **highlight feminism's inadequate recognition and marginalisation or even repression of differences among women, differences marked by power**. This form of feminist thought **questions any assumption of a (universalised) singular identity among women**, predicated on a shared experience of oppression.[4]

Such a brief statement of the broad features of feminist work attending to race/ethnicity does not, however, indicate its variations. Before delineating these features in more detail, it should be noted that some feminist commentators argue that the categories race and ethnicity are distinct and/or should be analysed separately. Nevertheless, many would assert that 'discrete definitions are not . . . easy to maintain' and that these categories are historically interwoven.[5] Indeed, certain contemporary feminist and other writers (particularly those aligned with postcolonialist/postnational/global and Third World themes) are inclined to reject a division between notions of race and ethnicity and suggest reference to the former be displaced in favour of the social constructivist associations they perceive in relation to 'ethnicity'. Such a position is disputed by other feminists engaged in this debate. In short, the theoretical relationship between the categories race and ethnicity is by no means clear-cut. By contrast, a relatively straightforward separation is generally maintained in the literature. Most writers concentrate on one or the other and rarely consider them both in the same piece of writing. This makes for something of a dilemma.

On balance I have decided to consider what can be seen as *points of intersection* between perspectives concentrating on race and those concerned with ethnicity within feminist thought and hence I refer to 'race/ethnicity' *in conjunction*. In other words, I neither assume the separation of the terms nor dissolve them into one. This decision grew out of an assessment of the difficulties associated with both these manoeuvres. On the one hand, I considered that there were some important overlaps between the terms and recognised the emerging significance of feminist theories which are inclined to perceive connections, such as 'postcolonial' feminist analyses. On the other hand, it seemed to me that persuasive arguments could be mounted against potentially de-emphasising the particular cultural histories of black and ethnic minority groups which might be associated with only employing the term ethnicity.[6] Indeed, my decision to focus on points of intersection maintains some of these problems in that it also reduces the historical and cultural specificities of the discussion and the extent to which the diversity and complexity of feminist work can be described. Such problems are not however limited to the focus of this chapter alone but are endemic in a relatively short book about feminist thought. I can only recommend, in relation to this chapter, that you might undertake additional reading, for example, to consider the ways in which writings which draw upon the struggles of various indigenous peoples might not intersect with those referring to 'cultures of migration'.[7]

The second point to make is that terms which refer to groups of people as 'black', 'white', 'ethnic' and so on, are used in a number of ways depending on the cultural context of the commentator. These terms are always political and locally differentiated. Moreover, in contemporary feminist writings on race/ethnicity these terms do not involve any conception of some innate/genetic (biological/'objective' scientific) basis for distinctions.[8] Although some groupings are relatively consistently associated with the term 'black' in Western societies, they may not be elsewhere, and many groupings are not even consistently described in the West. For instance, it is possible to be described as 'black' in the United Kingdom, and yet not be so described in the United States or Australia. My focus on points of intersection between feminist analyses of race and ethnicity avoids the difficulty of stating where the supposed boundaries between the social constitution of 'black' and particular 'ethnic' groupings might be, either in general in the West or in different Western societies. Additionally, this focus does not indicate who might (or might not) be generally regarded as marginalised by prevailing conceptions of 'race/ethnicity' in the West but rather simply uses specific examples from several Western countries.

REASSESSING (WHITE) FEMINISM

As stated earlier, contemporary Western feminists concerned with race/ethnicity critique the assumption of a common identity among women organised by a shared experience of subordination. This position is related to a **discernible shift in analyses expressing dissent from the dominant organisation of race/ethnicity around the 1960s and 1970s**. Prior to this, such analyses, including feminist ones, usually 'proceeded in an assimilationist manner' which presumed that the particularity of specific struggles should be subsumed within an overarching solidarity aimed at advancing humanity.⁹ Assimilationist perspectives rejected racial/ethnic stereotypes and argued for the *inclusion* of marginalised groups within the (liberal) project of universal human emancipation. In other words, they fought courageously for a recognition of similarity between those marginalised by racial/ethnic hierarchy and those marked as dominant on the basis of a shared humanity, for the right of the marginalised to be granted humanity. However, because this universalised emancipatory project relied upon a notion of what might be shared by all, what might be the same, it could not acknowledge differences to any great extent. Since differences are central to the political claims of groupings marginalised by a racial/ethnic hierarchy and to their very constitution/mobilisation as groupings (their cultural histories), assimilationist analyses were bound to offer rather undeveloped accounts of power and inadvertently reiterate the invisibility of the marginalised.

The limits of assimilationism gave way in feminist and other analyses to **a second phase predicated on an emphasis on anti-assimilation**. From around the 1960s–1970s, resistance to the dominant organisation of race/ethnicity was increasingly disentangled from an unproblematic acceptance of universalised accounts of emancipation. Anti-assimilationist analyses rejected *both* prevailing and feminist approaches which assumed either singularity/commonality/universality among all people (a universal human subject) or among all women (a universalised conception of women as a group). **Differences associated with marginalised racial/ethnic groupings were at least positively recognised or even strongly embraced.**

Feminist anti-assimilationist writers—that is, contemporary feminists concerned with race/ethnicity—thus offer a challenge to much of feminist thought because these writers refuse any presumption that women share a common identity based in a shared experience of oppression. They clearly indicate that social positioning cannot be universally understood only in terms of sexual difference.[10] These writers point out that the marginalisation or erasure of forms of differences which cannot be understood in terms of a dominant paradigm based on division between men and women means that many women's experiences will simply not be 'counted'.[11]

Anti-assimilationist feminists assert that, insomuch as feminist thought holds to a notion of women's commonality or common oppression, sexual difference is prioritised and other differences disappear. This leaves **white middle class women as the norm for what constitutes 'woman'** precisely *because* they are not marked by these other distracting distinctions. Ironically, white middle class women become the norm for women's group subordination as a consequence of their (comparative) privilege. In this context, Spelman notes, 'Black women's being Black somehow calls into question their counting as straightforward examples of "women", but white

women's being white does not'.[12] Contemporary feminists dealing with race/ethnicity assert that universalising procedures in
feminism reiterate racial/ethnic hierarchy and hence signal
feminism's complicity in racism/ethnocentrism.

The erasure of other differences is therefore not viewed as
a matter of simple analytical error but more as a highly
revealing slip. The unquestioning conception of women as
a group experiencing a shared subordination within much
feminist writing conveniently constructs all women as
disadvantaged—all are in some sense the victims rather than
the villains.[13] In this setting white women's implication in and
direct responsibility for racist oppression may be evaded.[14] The
representation of white middle class women as the norm for
women's oppression further obfuscates their investments in
power.

On the basis of this critique of feminism, feminists attending to race/ethnicity often refer to **white feminism**[15] and note
exclusions in its objects of theoretical analysis and political
practices. In making these points feminists dealing with
race/ethnicity draw upon the location of those positioned as
black/ethnic minority women. They note the characteristic
invisibility of race/ethnicity within feminism which is often or
even typically connected to the assumed equation of feminism
with a singular focus on sexual difference and with the celebration of a common 'sisterhood'. For example, race is
frequently conceived as something that can be simply *added on*
to this singular paradigm as an afterthought thereby rendering
black women as marginal within the paradigm because they are
ignored, romanticised or 'ghettoized' (regarded as representing
the particular or exceptional rather than the usual). It is no
surprise to find that the perception of such a consensus in
feminist thought is judged as successfully excluding the meaningful participation of black/ethnic minority women and
relatedly contributing to a perception by these women that
feminism is not 'for them'—because it does not advocate on
their behalf and because it is not a 'club' to which they would
be particularly keen to belong.[16]

Feminists concerned with race/ethnicity point out that
rendering black/ethnic minority women marginal within femi-

nism excludes recognition of the effects of differences between women. They argue that the concerns of white middle class women are not necessarily like those of black/ethnic minority women and that differences in the positioning of women are likely to produce very different—possibly incommensurable—problems and responses even in relation to the same issues. **hooks** cites the instance of white feminist perceptions of Madonna as subversive and suggests that Madonna's projection of sexual agency is scarcely of use to black women in the United States who may wish to refuse their representation as being sexually available.[17] Similarly, **Ang** argues that feminist slogans like 'when a woman says no, she means no', invoke qualities that are 'far from culturally neutral' in that they involve valuing 'individualism, conversational explicitness, directness and efficiency'.[18] Jolly and Martin outline the ways in which family, community and kinship—commonly criticised within feminism for their links with male dominance—cannot be perceived through a unitary lens and are likely to be differently experienced by white women as against women from the Pacific islands, or Aboriginal and migrant women in Australia.[19]

Even the paradigmatic exemplar of women's shared experience of oppression, rape, is regarded by **Behrendt** and **Huggins** as having different implications for different groups of women.[20] According to Huggins, rape cannot be simply understood as 'everybody's business'—that is, the rape of Australian Aboriginal women by Aboriginal men is not necessarily a subject appropriate for white feminists to discuss publicly and at a distance from the relevant Aboriginal communities in terms of men's brutal oppression of women. In her view this kind of discussion reinstates whites as the interpreters of Aboriginal experience while evading the significance of the context of racism in generating violence.

Feminists dealing with race/ethnicity point out that, in any case, **most issues faced by black/ethnic minority women are not readily comparable with those relevant to white women**, since the relationship between the two is structured by racism.[21] **O'Shane** notes the importance of literal survival issues for many Australian Aboriginal women related to racism.[22] A singular focus on what women have in common compared with men found in much feminist work cannot acknowledge experiences or political priorities such as survival which might be shared between men and women. In this context the claim that women are in much the same boat amounts to a refusal within feminist thought to come to grips not only with the different, even conflicting agendas of different women, but additionally with the **commonalities forged by racism/ethnocentrism and the strategic necessity for solidarity between men and women** to defend black/ethnic minority communities against racist/ethnocentrist practices.[23]

Such problems are raised by feminists dealing with race/ethnicity to alert feminists to the potential dangers of speaking on behalf of others, of speaking for women as if for all women.[24] And yet, this is frequently seen as feminism's agenda. If feminism cannot speak up for women, then does this amount to abandoning the feminist project of challenging male domination and women's marginality? Some writers attending to race/ethnicity announce the irrelevance of feminist thinking, describing it in discouraging terms as 'a family quarrel between white women and white men', and importantly raise concerns about its divisive impact on struggles undertaken in relation to racism/ethnocentrism.[25] However, the assessment of feminism as organised around a white norm and at a distance from many of the concerns of black/ethnic minority women by no means leads to an inevitable rejection of feminism *per se*, though feminism as it stands is typically rejected or strongly taken to task by those feminists engaged in race/ethnicity issues.

The critique such feminists offer regarding feminism's conception of women as a homogeneous group may be considered to arise out of too homogeneous an account of feminism itself, or at least an insufficiently detailed recognition of feminism's variety. Certainly the criticism of 'feminism' as if it were a unitary framework invites the question, 'which feminism?', or 'which aspects of feminism?' (The same problem arises in relation to postmodern/poststructuralist questioning of feminism.)

However, some feminists dealing with race/ethnicity also comment on specific approaches within feminism. These feminists direct their strongest criticisms at radical and liberal feminisms which they perceive as most clearly delivering the universalised and normative position which their overall critique of feminism outlines.[26] Radical feminists' insistence that sexual oppression is the most fundamental form of power and their related view that women have more in common with each other than they have with any man, is perceived as exemplifying authoritarian claims which feminists of race/ethnicity wish to disavow. Feminists concerned with race/ethnicity draw attention to the solidarity created between men and women who experience racism/ethnocentrism and, in asserting this commonality, they sometimes pose race/ethnicity as the more fundamental form of power. More often feminists attending to race/ethnicity simply question the notion of oppression that is so central to radical feminism insofar as they question the degree of oppression suffered by white women. They note the multiple effects of power on women who are constituted as racially/ethnically 'Other' and never positioned as dominant.[27] In relation to liberal feminism, feminists dealing with race/ethnicity raise criticisms regarding its positive valuation of individualism, acceptance of class differentiation, and distaste for radical change.

TRAJECTORIES: IDENTITY POLITICS AND A SOCIAL CONSTRUCTIVIST POLITICS OF DIFFERENCE

It was stated earlier that feminist and other analyses which dissented from the dominant organisation of race/ethnicity moved from assimilationism towards an anti-assimilationist framework around the 1960s to 1970s. Two major trajectories *within* this anti-assimilationist stance may be detected: one based on **identity politics** and the other on **a newly emerging social constructivism or cultural politics of difference**. These trajectories are not necessarily antagonistic and in many ways they coexist and/or overlap (sometimes in the work of a single author).[28] They involve the development of forms of politics organised around black/ethnic minority identity and in relation to black/ethnic minority women. Such trajectories are sometimes perceived in terms of a **shift in black/ethnic minority politics with identity politics receding and a cultural politics of difference on the rise**.[29] Both attack singular universalising procedures in relation to notions of humanity and to women by referring to racial/ethnic differences but they offer relatively more or less strong accounts of those differences and more or less critical perspectives with regard to the category race/ethnicity. These forms of anti-assimilationist analysis diverge in their assessment of differences related to race/ethnicity which are viewed as either virtually incommensurable or as unstable and relatively fluid. They also differ in their willingness to apply the critique of universalism to black/ethnic minority identities. One form views these identities in terms of common struggle and continuity of experience, while the other is concerned with deconstructing assumptions regarding commonality among black or ethnic minority groupings.

The trajectory I have described as 'identity politics' stresses the marked historical/cultural differences between black/ethnic minority and white communities, differences which are so sharp as to frequently involve conflicting 'interests'. Additionally, this politics takes up marginalised racial/ethnic identities and challenges racism/ethnocentrism by evaluating these identities positively. Generally those advocating identity politics insist that, despite the dangers of appearing to replicate assumptions linked to subordination, people/women within black and ethnic minority groups are indeed alike:[30] they do actually have a common identity, common experience, which may be related to cultural origins as well as being constituted by specific forms of racism/ethnocentrism. On this ground they suggest an at least strategic acceptance of group identities referring to black/ethnic minority communities and/or black/ethnic minority women as a self-evident existing basis for mobilising political solidarity. The critique of universalism and espousal of difference mounted in relation to social categories other than race/ethnicity is not applied to marginalised black/ethnic identities, at least in part because the weight of dominant negative assessments regarding these identities is judged to be so overwhelming that inversion of these assessments is seen as a critical priority. It is hoped by those supporting identity politics that a positive valuation of marginalised identities will enable those who are marginalised to draw strength from such a valuation.

Identity politics within feminist writings on race/ethnicity involves emphasising the significant, even incommensurable, differences between black and white women and stressing the existence of a coherent black or, at minimum, black female identity.[31] Because of the coherence assumed in relation to marginalised racial/ethnic identities, feminist accounts of identity politics dealing with race/ethnicity tend to hold to distinctions between categories and thus prefer to employ separate terminologies referring to race and ethnicity.[32] Such distinctions also provide a location for descriptions of different but interlocking (not shared) oppressions, usefully described by King as 'multiple jeopardy'.[33] The conception of interlocking oppressions encourages two potentially connected versions of the interplay between the categories sex and race/ethnicity (as well as their intersection with other categories) which both depict a feminism which is comparatively limited in its claims and does not assume it is an obvious political home for all women. The first envisages feminism as organised around the principle of solidarity or coalition between different women (a political community) usually around specific problems but also in some longer term sense.[34] The second proposes a more restricted role for feminism and argues for a separate struggle against racism/ethnocentrism given ongoing doubts about assimilationist tendencies in existing feminism. Nevertheless, some writers who might, for instance, recommend an autonomous anti-racist or black women's movement,[35] also support the conception of feminism as a coalition. bell hooks remarks that although some feminists now feel that any form of unity is impossible because of differences between women:

> . . . [a]bandoning the idea of sisterhood as an expression of political solidarity weakens and diminishes the feminist movement . . . There can be no mass-based feminist movement to end sexist oppression without a united front . . . Women are enriched when

we bond with one another . . . We can bond on the basis of our political commitment to a feminist movement.[36]

The second trajectory associated with anti-assimilationism has been described in terms of a new social constructivism or cultural politics of difference. Here, instead of the attack on universalising notions of commonality stopping at the door of the category race/ethnicity, the innocence of conceptions of black/ethnic minority groups or of women being all the same is rejected. Differences within these groups and among black/ethnic minority women are not suppressed. Hence this politics of difference does not straightforwardly value black/ethnic minority identities as positive: there is no simple celebration of these identities as good.[37] Rather than claiming and positively valuing identities associated with race/ethnicity, the emphasis is instead upon their socially constructed character and the rejection of any essential foundation for these identities. On this basis the term race may be displaced by ethnicity, given that the former suggests irreducible differences guaranteed by biology. Nevertheless, ethnicity is also judged to be a term that needs to be shorn of its essentialist connotations and its use is distinguished from any assumption of fixed cultural identity or overly respectful view of cultural integrity.[38]

By comparison with identity politics the more thorough-going constructivism of this politics of difference questions the self-evident unity and commonality of racial/ethnic identities. Those supporting a politics of difference are consequently less vociferous regarding distinctions such as black/white, pointing out that the distinction makes invisible those who do not fit neatly into either of its categories.[39] Such categories are treated as more unstable and fluid than identity politics might allow.[40] In this context, feminist accounts of the politics of difference note that racism/ethnocentrism operates precisely to construct impassable and naturalised boundaries between groups defined by race/ethnicity. Gayatri **Spivak,** for instance, problematises categories which constitute marginalised racial/ethnic groups as the 'Other', as distinct and opposite from the dominant norm, and refers to the 'epistemic violence' of the socially constructed representations thrown up by imperialism and nationalism as well as those linked with notions of the primitive and exotic.[41] These categories are also connected with the effects of the social organisation of black/ethnic 'diaspora communities'[42] and the colonisation of indigenous peoples. In these senses the feminist employment of a new cultural politics of difference is strongly attached to what is often termed **'postcolonial'**[43] and to a lesser extent to certain forms of multiculturalism—that is, it is concerned to engage with, but also deconstruct, difference by destabilising assumptions about what is core (the norm) and what lies at the periphery (designated as other) in a postcolonial (post-imperialist) world marked by waves of migration. As against fixed notions of separate and hierarchical racial/ethnic identities there is some uncertainty about a celebratory 'fetishization' of difference and 'Otherness'.[44] However, despite the interest of feminists developing a cultural politics of difference in the postmodern agenda of destabilising identity, they generally do not display as unreserved a determination to demonstrate the fluidity of identity, especially of identities linked to race/ethnicity. Additionally, they often express doubts about the extent to which social relations can be described in postmodern terms.[45]

To summarise, the critique of universalising procedures in relation to women as a group is expressed in all variations of contemporary feminist work dealing with race/ethnicity. Although this potentially places them on similar ground to the views of postmodern/poststructuralist thinkers, feminist work on race/ethnicity does not necessarily reject macro forms of analysis or centralised explanatory principles, particularly in relation to race/ethnicity. In Spivak's terms the postmodern critique of universalising categories may not always be followed relentlessly.[46] For instance, feminists attending to race are not usually convinced that identity, in the sense of belonging to an oppressed group, can or should be substantially disaggregated. Moreover, this form of feminism is less inclined to welcome suggestions that a singular identity (such as being black) be abandoned in favour of a plurality of identities and multiple points of resistance.[47] Reservations regarding this plurality appear to be linked to concern that it may imitate a form of cultural genocide. Lastly, feminists concentrating on race/ethnicity have some points of connection with Marx-ist/socialist feminism insofar as both are insistent on the several (if not plural) modalities of power. Nonetheless, the former grouping remains sceptical that the Marxist/socialist feminist tradition can consider race/ethnicity as anything but an after-thought to be added on to an analytical framework that is built around class and sex.[48]

The critique of feminism and its various forms offered by feminists attending to race/ethnicity involves reassessing femi-nist thought. Such reassessments are very much a part of contemporary feminist approaches and at the same time they signal potential future directions for feminism. In this sense this last chapter can function as a means to refresh your memory concerning feminism's characteristics, as well as a means by which you might contemplate your own response to the question 'what *is* feminism?', before moving on to the book's brief conclusion.

Conclusion

The point of a book like this is that there can be no final answer to the question, 'what is feminism anyway?'. A number of characteristics may be recognised but even these may not be set or certain in any eternal sense. Hence, it is more appropriate to describe these characteristics as indicators of feminist thought thus far than as permanent markers. In this setting, I suggested initially that feminist thought involves a critical response to traditional theorising which thereby alters what may be discussed and how it may be discussed. That critique challenges assumptions of male supremacy/centrality.

Additional characteristics include the following:

- a focus on considering women as the subject of the analysis which may involve attention to differences within/between women and in any case is not necessarily exclusive;
- several typical debates—especially around whether feminism has or should have an abiding core, the degree of social change envisaged, and the extent to which feminism 'belongs' to women to the exclusion of men;
- an inclination to propose how things ought or ought not be, revolving around resistance to power and the privileging of men;
- an at least minimal group rather than individual orientation; and,
- finally, a certain selection (seven are described in this book) of identifiable approaches.

(This last requirement indicates that one way of describing feminism is simply to refer to its several expressions. Feminism can be seen as the sum of these parts.)

But at this juncture it becomes evident that feminism exceeds both the mundane listing of its characteristics and of its summarised 'types'. It has an incremental quality that is not so easily reducible and one aspect of this arises in relation to its 'felt' connotations. Though this aspect is often not acknowledged, feminism can also be associated with an emotional attachment for those who claim membership within it. This may seem an odd thing to mention after you, the reader, have slogged your way through a book which presents feminism as an intellectual field. However, precisely because theory and its abstract form are frequently conceived as rather 'dry', I consider that it is very important to stress that feminist thought, even at its most abstract, may be identified by its 'text appeal'.[1] It is not a field that is emotionally neutral for its 'membership', for those who are ambivalent about its attractions, or for its detractors. In the case of those who see themselves as part of feminism or at least as engaged with it, their relation to it is rather like a love affair which, whether long term or not, amounts to a demanding, intense investment. That affair is sometimes wrenching, often tiring, but it is nevertheless desired. As a conversation between several feminists published in the journal *Ms.* indicates, feminism can produce pleasure:

> I think we need to talk about the joy. I get such joy out of feminism. It is the greatest joy of my life, and somehow we don't translate that. (Gloria Steinem)[2]

And since 'mainstream' society's conceptions of feminism are inclined to repress this possibility, why not end the feminist story with a happy ending, just for once.

Notes

INTRODUCTION

1 My source for this form of question is found in Richard Johnson's 1983 article, 'What is cultural studies anyway?', *Estratto da Anglistica*, xxvi, 1–2, Istituto Universitario Orientale, Naples.
2 J. Stacey, 'Untangling feminist theory' in *Introducing Women's Studies*, eds D. Richardson and V. Robinson, Macmillan, London, 1993, p. 73; A. Curthoys, 'Australian feminism since 1970' in *Australian Women: Contemporary Feminist Thought*, eds N. Grieve and A. Burns, Oxford University Press, Melbourne, 1994, pp. 18–19.
3 D. Thompson, 'Defining feminism', *Australian Feminist Studies*, no. 20, Summer 1994, pp. 171–2.
4 R. Braidotti, *Patterns of Dissonance: A Study of Women in Contemporary Philosophy*, Polity Press, Cambridge, 1991, p. 147.
5 A. Jardine, *Gynesis: Configurations of Woman and Modernity*, Cornell University Press, Ithaca and London, 1985, p. 20.
6 P. Rothfield, 'New wave feminism: feminism and postmodernism' in *Discourse and Difference: Poststructuralism, Feminism and the Moment of History*, eds A. Milner and C. Worth, Centre for General and Comparative Literature (Monash University), Clayton, Victoria, 1990, p. 94.
7 K. Offen, 'Defining feminism: a comparative historical approach', *Signs*, vol. 14, no. 1, Autumn 1988, p. 126; see also entry under 'Feminism' in L. Tuttle, *Encyclopedia of Feminism*, Arrow Books, London, 1986, pp. 107–8.
8 Offen, ibid., pp. 128–32; B. Caine, 'Women's studies, feminist traditions and the problem of history' in *Transitions: New Australian Feminisms*, eds B. Caine and R. Pringle, Allen & Unwin, Sydney, 1995, p. 2.

119

9   R. Delmar, 'What is feminism?' in *What is Feminism?*, eds J. Mitchell and A. Oakley, Basil Blackwell, Oxford, 1986, pp. 8–33.
10 ibid., pp. 8–9.
11 See D. Thompson, 'Defining Feminism', p. 172.
12 See E. Gross (Grosz), 'What is feminist theory?' in *Feminist Challenges: Social and Political Theory*, eds C. Pateman and E. Gross, Allen & Unwin, Sydney, pp. 190–204. (Australian philosopher, Elizabeth Grosz, published under the name of Gross before the late 1980s. For the sake of consistency hereafter I will always refer to her as Grosz, except in the rare circumstance when this might mislead and prevent a reader from finding a reference, such as when she is a co-author of a book.)
13 Braidotti, *Patterns of Dissonance*, p. 147.

CHAPTER 1

1   C. Pateman and M. Shanley, 'Introduction' in *Feminist Interpretations and Political Theory*, eds M. Shanley and C. Pateman, Polity Press, Cambridge, 1991, pp. 1–10; J. Grimshaw, *Feminist Philosophers: Women's Perspectives on Philosophical Traditions*, Harvester Wheatsheaf, Hemel Hempstead, Hertfordshire, 1986, pp. 36–74; C. Pateman, 'Introduction: The theoretical subversiveness of feminism' in *Feminist Challenges: Social and Political Theory*, eds C. Pateman and E. Gross, Allen & Unwin, Sydney, 1986, pp. 1–10; E. Grosz, 'Conclusion: What is feminist theory?' in *Feminist Challenges*, ibid., p. 190.
2   M. O'Brien, *The Politics of Reproduction*, RKP, London, 1981, p. 5.
3   For example we could compare the content of discipline based theoretical journals like *Journal of Politics* with that of feminist journals like *Signs* and *Australian Feminist Studies*.
4   Pateman, 'Introduction' in *Feminist Challenges*, p. 6.
5   A. March in 'Female Invisibility in Androcentric Sociological Theory', *Insurgent Sociologist*, vol. 11, no. 2, 1982, pp. 99–107, outlines a number of mechanisms which render women invisible in sociology. See also B. Theile, 'Vanishing acts in social and political thought: Tricks of the trade' in *Feminist Challenges*, pp. 33–4 and 42; Grimshaw, *Feminist Philosophers*, pp. 52–4.
6   Thiele, ibid., p. 30.
7   Mary Wollstonecraft is generally viewed as the major Liberal feminist thinker of the eighteenth century (1759–97) and as such she is more likely to be found in conventional courses on political

theory and the history of political philosophy than any other feminist theorist. Since Wollstonecraft is already likely to be recognised by the mainstream, adding her work to academic courses as a means of including thinking about women in the range of ideas on social and political life is a realistic option. See Grimshaw, *Feminist Philosophers*, pp. 10–11.

8 L. Clark and L. Lange, *The Sexism of Social and Political Theory*, University of Toronto Press, Toronto, 1979, p. xvii.

9 E. Grosz, 'The in(ter)vention of feminist knowledges' in *Crossing Boundaries: Feminisms and the Critique of Knowledges*, eds B. Caine *et al.*, Allen & Unwin, Sydney, 1988, p. 99; Grosz, 'Conclusion' in *Feminist Challenges*, p. 197; M. Gatens, 'Feminism, philosophy and riddles without answers' in *Feminist Challenges*, pp. 25–9.

10 *Advertiser*, Tuesday March 3, 1992, 'Appeal' section, p. 2.

11 Grimshaw, *Feminist Philosophers*, p. 69.

12 E. Porter, *Women and Moral Identity*, Allen & Unwin, Sydney, 1991, pp. 55–8. (Also A. March and B. Theile, see note 5 in this chapter).

13 Porter, ibid., p. 55.

14 Porter, ibid., p.56; Aristotle, *Politics*, Book 1, ch. 13, trans. T. Sinclair, Penguin Books, London, 1972, p. 52; see also A. Saxonhouse, 'On Aristotle' in *Feminist Interpretations and Political Theory*, p.38 and M. Gatens, 'The dangers of a woman-centred philosophy' in *The Polity Reader in Gender Studies*, Polity, Cambridge, 1994, p. 99.

15 E. Porter, *Women and Moral Identity*, p. 56.

16 ibid., p. 57; see also Gatens, 'The dangers of a woman-centred philosophy', p. 98–9.

17 E. Porter, *Women and Moral Identity*, p. 57; S. de Beauvoir, *The Second Sex*, trans. and ed. H. Parshley, Penguin Books, London, 1975, p. 16; see also E. Spelman, 'On de Beauvoir' in *Feminist Interpretations and Political Theory*, pp. 200–3.

18 E. Porter, *Women and Moral Identity*, p. 58; C. Pateman, *The Sexual Contract*, Polity, Oxford, 1988, pp. 96–102; S. Moller-Okin, 'Rousseau's natural woman', *Journal of Politics*, no. 41, 1979, p. 401.

19 Grimshaw makes a similar point. Grimshaw, *Feminist Philosophers*, p. 34.

20 J. Derrida, *Positions*, University of Chicago Press, Chicago, 1981, p. 41.

21 Many feminist theorists have referred to and listed dualisms in Western thinking. See for example H. Cixous, 'Sorties' in *New*

French Feminisms: An Anthology, eds E. Marks and I. de Courtivron, Harvester Press, Sussex, 1981, pp. 90–1; E. Porter, *Women and Moral Identity*, p. 51. I have also paid attention to a list provided by Chilla Bulbeck at a 'Reshaping Australian Institutions' conference, Australian National University, 1995.

CHAPTER 2

1 J. Richards, *The Sceptical Feminist: A Philosophical Enquiry*, Penguin, Harmondsworth, 1982.
2 C. Pateman, 'Introduction: The theoretical subversiveness of feminism' in *Feminist Challenges: Social and Political Theory*, eds C. Pateman and E. Gross, Allen & Unwin, Sydney, 1986, pp. 4–5.
3 Pateman, ibid., p. 6; C. Pateman and M. Shanley, 'Introduction' in *Feminist Interpretations and Political Theory*, eds M. Shanley and C. Pateman, Polity Press, Cambridge, 1991, p. 3; C. Pateman, *The Sexual Contract*, Polity, Oxford, 1988, p. x.
4 See E. Grosz, 'Conclusion: what is feminist theory?' in *Feminist Challenges: Social and Political Theory*, eds C. Pateman and E. Gross, Allen & Unwin, Sydney, 1986, pp. 193 and 195–6.
5 ibid., pp. 190–204; P. Rothfield, 'New wave feminism: feminism and postmodernism' in *Discourse and Difference: Poststructuralism, Feminism and the Moment of History*, eds A. Milner and C. Worth, Centre for General and Comparative Literature (Monash University), Clayton, Victoria, 1990, pp. 96–7.
6 Here I have both drawn upon and reworked certain aspects of the work of Elizabeth Grosz. E. Grosz, 'Conclusion: what is feminist theory?' in *Feminist Challenges*, pp. 190–204; E. Grosz, 'The in(ter)vention of feminist knowledges' in *Crossing Boundaries: Feminisms and the Critique of Knowledges*, eds B. Caine et al., Allen & Unwin, Sydney, 1988, pp. 92–104.
7 See Iris Young, 'Humanism, gynocentrism and feminist politics', *Women's Studies International Forum*, vol. 8, no. 3, 1985.
8 A. Summers, 'Feminism on two continents: the women's movement in Australia and the United States' in *Australian Women: Contemporary Feminist Thought*, eds N. Grieve and A. Burns, Oxford University Press, Melbourne, 1994, pp. 53–8; J. Lattas, 'French Feminisms' in *Social Theory: A Guide to Central Thinkers*, ed. P. Beilharz, Allen & Unwin, 1991, pp. 99–100.
9 I. Young, 'Humanism, gynocentrism and feminist politics'.
10 J. Lattas, 'French Feminisms', p. 99; G. Spivak, 'French feminism

in an international frame', *Yale French Studies*, no. 62, 1981, p. 179; C. Bacchi, *Same Difference: Feminism and Sexual Difference*, Allen & Unwin, Sydney, 1990, pp. x–xx.

11 While it can be said that French feminists (of the school 'écriture feminine') are also involved in a critique of the sameness/difference dichotomy (see Gatens), their approach more clearly offers a challenge to some aspects of this opposition rather than refusing the dichotomy entirely. They remain in my view under the auspices of a 'difference' perspective insofar as they celebrate the strategic potentialities of femininity and the feminine body in exemplifying Otherness. M. Gatens, 'Power, Bodies and Difference' in *Destabilizing Theory: Contemporary Feminist Debates*, eds M. Barrett and A. Phillips, Polity, Cambridge, 1992, pp. 133–5; M. Barrett and A. Phillips, 'Introduction' in *Destabilizing Theory*, p. 8.

12 C. MacKinnon, *Feminism Unmodified: Discourses on Life and Law*, Harvard University Press, Cambridge, 1987, p. 40; for an Australian version of MacKinnon's approach, see D. Thompson, 'Defining feminism', *Australian Feminist Studies*, no. 20, Summer 1994, pp. 186–7; J. Scott, 'Deconstructing equality–versus–difference: or, the uses of postructuralist theory for feminism', *Feminist Studies*, vol. 14, no. 33, pp. 33–50, 1988, p. 48; R. Graycar and J. Morgan, *The Hidden Gender of Law*, The Federation Press, Sydney, 1990, pp. 47–50.

13 B. Reagon, 'Coalition politics: turning the century' in *Home Girls: A Black Feminist Anthology*, ed. B. Smith, Kitchen Table/Women of Colour Press, N.Y., 1983, pp. 356–68; A. Curthoys, 'Australian Feminism since 1970' in *Australian Women*, p. 26; J. Huggins, 'A contemporary view of Aboriginal women's relationship to the white women's movement' in *Australian Women*, pp. 70–9.

14 Indeed, some feminists strongly contest any conception of feminism as being solely about women. See b. hooks, quoted in 'Let's get real about feminism: the backlash, the myths, the movement', *Ms.*, vol. iv, no. 2, September/October, 1993, pp. 37–8.

15 R. Delmar, 'What is Feminism?' in *What is Feminism?*, eds J. Mitchell and A. Oakley, Basil Blackwell, Oxford, 1986, pp. 22 and 28.

16 ibid., pp. 26–8. Delmar refers to feminists who make use of psychoanalysis, critical theory and deconstruction when she is discussing those who are suspicious of the concept of woman (p. 28). See also C. Bulbeck, 'First and Third World feminisms', *Asian Studies Review*, vol. 15, no. 1, July 1991, pp. 77–91.

17 D. Riley, *Am I That Name?: Feminism and the Category of 'Women'
    in History*, Macmillan, Basingstoke, 1988, p. 5.

18 Delmar, 'What is feminism?', pp. 10–11.

19 Thompson insists that the process of defining feminism does not
    fix its meaning but rather sets up useful dialogue, and in conse-
    quence she sees no difficulty in providing a 'clear and
    unambiguous account of what feminism is'. She may have a point
    about the task of definition, but for me, at least, clarity is not
    necessarily accompanied by the dissolution of ambiguity. Further-
    more, while the explicit purpose of Thompson's analysis is to
    locate her own standpoint, my main interest in this book is to
    outline the variety of ways in which feminism is understood to
    enable the reader to peruse the field. Thompson, 'Defining
    feminism', pp. 172–3.

20 ibid., p. 173.

21 Some postmodern feminists, following Lyotard and Foucault,
    consider that the assertion of authoritative knowledge contains
    the problem of replicating hierarchical ways of thinking present
    in mainstream thought. I agree, but consider that there are other
    choices than simply those of hierarchical authority or silence. In
    this setting, the question for me is more *how* one speaks about
    feminism, how one goes about the task of definition, and not
    whether or not this task should be attempted. I, like Gallop, see
    certain advantages in explicitly asserting a position on the subject
    of feminism. J. Gallop, *Reading Lacan*, Cornell University Press,
    Ithaca, 1985, p. 21; for an interesting analysis of this debate, see
    also P. Rothfield, 'New wave feminism: feminism and
    postmodernism' in *Discourse and Difference: Poststructuralism, Femi-
    nism and the Moment of History*, eds A. Milner and C. Worth, Centre
    for General and Comparative Literature (Monash University),
    Clayton, Victoria, 1990.

CHAPTER 3

1 E. Grosz, 'Conclusion: what is feminist theory?' in *Feminist
   Challenges: Social and Political Theory*, eds C. Pateman and E. Gross,
   Allen & Unwin, Sydney, 1986, pp. 193–6.

2 L. Tuttle, *Encyclopedia of Feminism*, Arrow Books, London, 1987,
   p. 107.

3 N. Abercrombie *et al.*, *The Penguin Dictionary of Sociology*, 2nd edn,
   Penguin, London, 1988, p. 96.

4   D. Robertson, *The Penguin Dictionary of Politics*, 2nd edn, Penguin, London, 1993, p. 186, emphasis in original.

5   J. Grimshaw, *Feminist Philosophers: Women's Perspectives on Philosophical Traditions*, Wheatsheaf Books, Brighton, 1986, p. 20.

6   E. Porter, *Women and Moral Identity*, Allen & Unwin, Sydney, 1991, p. 5.

7   R. Delmar, 'What is feminism?' in *What is Feminism?*, eds J. Mitchell and A. Oakley, Basil Blackwell, Oxford, 1986, p. 9.

8   V. George and P. Wilding, *Ideology and Social Welfare*, RKP, London, 1976, p. 44, quoted in L. Bryson, *Welfare and the State: Who Benefits?*, Macmillan, London, 1992.

9   Grosz, 'Conclusion: What is feminist theory?', p. 196; Delmar, 'What is feminism?', pp. 12–13.

10 M. Barrett and A. Phillips, 'Introduction' in *Destabilizing Theory: Contemporary Feminist Debates*, eds M. Barrett and A. Phillips, Polity, Cambridge, 1992, pp. 2–7.

11 S. Bordo, 'Feminism, postmodernism and gender scepticism' in *Feminism/Postmodernism*, ed. L. Nicholson, Routledge, London, 1990, p. 149.

12 J. Grant, *Fundamental Feminism: Contesting the Core Concepts of Feminist Theory*, Routledge, London, 1993, pp. 1–4.

13 b. hooks, quoted in Tuttle, *Encyclopedia of Feminism*, p. 107; see b. hooks, *Feminist Theory: From Margin to Center*, South End Press, 1984.

14 b. hooks, interview in 'Let's get real about feminism: the backlash, the myths, the movement', *Ms.*, vol. iv, no. 2, September–October 1993, p. 42, see also p. 41.

15 N. Wolf, interview in 'Let's get real about feminism', pp. 41–3.

16 A. Jaggar, quoted in Tuttle, *Encyclopedia of Feminism*, p. 107; see A. Jaggar, *Feminist Politics and Human Nature*, Rowman & Allanheld, Totowa, N.J., 1983.

17 Davies expresses more explicitly an assumption regularly found in dictionary definitions. M. Davies, *Asking the Law Question*, The Law Book Company, Sydney, 1994, p. 172.

18 See, for example, the avoidance of the reform/revolution divide in R. Pringle and S. Watson, '"Women's interests" and the poststructuralist state' in *Destabilizing Theory*, pp. 53–73; R. Felski, 'American and British feminisms' in *Social Theory: A Guide to Central Thinkers*, ed. P. Beilharz, Allen & Unwin, Sydney, 1991, p. 22.

19 Barrett and Phillips, 'Introduction', pp. 6–7.

20 Delmar, 'What is feminism?', p. 27.

21 ibid.
22 hooks, 'Let's get real about feminism', p. 37; G. Spivak, 'The politics of translation' in *Destabilizing Theory*, p. 192.
23 hooks, ibid., pp. 37–8.

CHAPTER 4

1 The kinds of debate outlined previously may themselves be considered part of what can be identified as feminist.
2 No writings identified with feminist concerns accept the status quo with regard to the positioning of women and hence all at some level assume that this positioning *ought* to change.
3 Delmar among others stresses the plurality of feminism's interpretive frameworks but, as is commonly the case, pays little attention to methodological dilemmas. R. Delmar, 'What is feminism?' in *What is Feminism?*, eds J. Mitchell and A. Oakley, Basil Blackwell, Oxford, 1986, p. 9.
4 b. hooks, *Feminist Theory: From Margin to Center*, South End Press, 1984; N. Wolf, *Fire with Fire: The New Female Power and How It Will Change the 21st Century*, Chatto & Windus, London, 1993; C. Mohanty, 'Feminist encounters: locating the politics of experience' in *Destabilizing Theory: Contemporary Feminist Debates*, eds M. Barrett and A. Phillips, Polity, Cambridge, 1992, pp. 84–9; R. Pringle and S. Watson, '"Women's Interests" and the poststructuralist state' in *Destabilizing Theory*, ibid. pp. 68–70.
5 See bell hooks, chapter 3, notes 21 and 22 and N. Wolf, 'How to be a feminist and still love men', *Cleo*, February, 1993, pp. 71 and 142.
6 K. Offen, 'Defining feminism: a comparative historical approach', *Signs*, vol. 14, no. 1, Autumn 1988, pp. 134–6.
7 E. Grosz, 'Conclusion: What is feminist theory?' in *Feminist Challenges: Social and Political Theory*, eds C. Pateman and E. Gross, Allen & Unwin, Sydney, 1986, pp. 190–204; E. Grosz, 'The in(ter)vention of feminist knowledges' in *Crossing Boundaries: Feminisms and the Critique of Knowledges*, eds B. Caine *et al.*, Allen & Unwin, Sydney, 1988, pp. 92–104. See also Gatens' use of the same distinction between 'equality' and 'difference' feminisms. M. Gatens, 'Power, bodies and difference' in *Destabilizing Theory*, p. 135.
8 Offen, 'Defining feminism', p. 132.
9 J. Elshtain, *Public Man, Private Woman*, Princeton University Press,

Princeton, 1981; A. Jaggar, *Feminist Politics and Human Nature*, Harvester Press, Sussex, 1983; J. Donovan, *Feminist Theory*, Unger, N.Y., 1985; R. Tong, *Feminist Thought: A Comprehensive Introduction*, 1st edn, Unwin Hyman, London, 1989; R. Tong, *Feminist Thought: A More Comprehensive Introduction*, 2nd edn, Allen & Unwin, Sydney, 1998.

10 'Existentialist feminism' is not included as a tradition or school because this term largely describes the influence of one writer, Simone de Beauvoir, and one text, *The Second Sex*. Existentialism seems to me more an influence within, rather than a category of, feminism. S. de Beauvoir, *The Second Sex*, trans. and ed. H. Parshley, Vintage Books, N.Y., 1974. For a commentary on 'existentialist feminism' see Tong, *Feminist Thought*, 1st edn, pp. 195–216 or Tong, *Feminist Thought*, 2nd edn, pp. 173–92.

11 J. Stacey, 'Untangling feminist theory' in *Introducing Women's Studies: Feminist Theory and Practice*, eds D. Richardson and V. Robinson, Macmillan, London, 1993, pp. 49–73.

12 J. Green, *Fundamental Feminism: Contesting the Core Concepts of Feminist Theory*, Routledge, N.Y., 1993, p. 4.

CHAPTER 5

1 M. Tapper, 'Can a feminist be a liberal?', *Australasian Journal of Philosophy*, no. 64, Supplement, June 1986, pp. 37–47.

2 N. Wolf, *Fire with Fire: The New Female Power and How It Will Change the 21st Century*, Chatto & Windus, London, 1993, pp. xvii–xix; also *The Beauty Myth*, Chatto & Windus, London, 1990. For a comment on Wolf's North American and relatively conservative positioning from another liberal feminist, see B. Faust, 'Australian-style feminism: what a gift to the world', *Australian*, 22 February, 1994.

3 This form of liberalism is also sometimes described as 'small l' liberalism or 'political liberalism'. Welfare liberals may be referred to as 'wets'. See L. Bryson, *Welfare and the State: Who Benefits?*, Macmillan, London, 1992, pp. 39–46.

4 J.S. Mill (1806–73) was an English philosopher, essayist, economist and parliamentarian. He is arguably the single most influential man in the history of Western feminist thought. See D. Robertson, *The Penguin Dictionary of Politics*, 2nd edn, Penguin, London, 1993, pp. 314–5; L. Tuttle, *Encyclopedia of Feminism*, Arrow Books, London, 1987, p. 205.

5 *Laissez-faire* liberalism (also known as market or economic liberalism) is linked to the work of economic and political theorists such as Adam Smith and Jeremy Bentham rather than that of J.S. Mill. It is associated with 'dry' New Right economics. See Bryson, *Welfare and the State*; also H. Stretton and L. Orchard, *Public Goods, Public Enterprise, Public Choice: Theoretical Foundations of the Contemporary Attack on Government*, Macmillan/St Martin's Press, London, N.Y., 1994, pp. 252–8.

6 A. Curthoys, 'Australian feminism since 1970' in *Australian Women: Contemporary Feminist Thought*, eds N. Grieve and A. Burns, Oxford University Press, Melbourne, 1994, p. 25; M. Sawer, 'Feminism and the state; Australia compared', seminar paper delivered to the Department of Politics, University of Adelaide, May 1992; M. Sawer, 'Why has the women's movement had more influence on government in Australia than elsewhere?' in *Australia Compared: People, Policies and Politics*, ed. F. Castles, Allen & Unwin, Sydney, 1991, pp. 258–77; H. Eisenstein, *Gender Shock: Practising Feminism on Two Continents*, Allen & Unwin, Sydney, 1991.

7 Z. Eisenstein, *The Radical Future of Liberal Feminism*, North Eastern University Press, Boston, 1986; S. Wendell, 'A (qualified) defense of liberal feminism', *Hypatia*, vol. 2, no. 2, Summer 1987, pp. 65–94; R. Tong, *Feminist Thought: A Comprehensive Introduction*, 1st edn, Unwin Hyman, London, 1989, pp. 11–38 or R. Tong, *Feminist Thought: A More Comprehensive Introduction*, 2nd edn, Allen & Unwin, Sydney, 1998, pp. 10–44.

8 R. Rowland and R. Klein, 'Radical feminism: critique and construct' in *Feminist Knowledge: Critique and Construct*, ed. S. Gunew, Routledge, London and N.Y., 1990, pp. 272–5, 280 and 282.

9 Sonia Johnson, quoted in Rowland and Klein, ibid. p. 281.

10 A. Rich, 'Compulsory heterosexuality and lesbian existence', *Signs*, vol. 5, no. 4, Summer 1980, pp. 631–60.

11 D. Thompson, 'Defining feminism', *Australian Feminist Studies*, no. 20, Summer 1994, p.177.

12 T. Atkinson, *Amazon Odyssey*, Links Books, N.Y., 1974, p. 73.

13 K. Millett, *Sexual Politics*, Avon Books, N.Y., 1971.

14 See section on 'The patriarchy debate' in J. Stacey, 'Untangling feminist theory' in *Introducing Women's Studies: Feminist theory and practice*, eds D. Richardson and V. Robinson, Macmillan, London, 1993, pp. 52–9.

15 R. Morgan, *Going Too Far*, Vintage Books, N.Y., 1978, p. 13.

16 See for example, R. Morgan, *Sisterhood is Global*, Anchor Press/Doubleday, N.Y., 1984; Atkinson, *Amazon Odyssey*, pp. 46–55.

17 C. Delphy, 'The main enemy' in C. Delphy, *Close to Home: A Materialist Analysis of Women's Oppression*, trans. and ed. D. Leonard, Hutchinson, London, 1984, pp. 57–77. (This paper was first published in 1970, and in English in 1974.)

18 Rowland and Klein, 'Radical feminism', p. 280.

19 Thompson, 'Defining feminism', p. 173.

20 Both Ti-Grace Atkinson and Shulemith Firestone argue that the original cause of male domination resides in men's ability to take advantage of women's social vulnerability related to the latter's reproductive capacities. Atkinson, *Amazon Odyssey*; S. Firestone, *The Dialectic of Sex: The Case for Feminist Revolution*, Bantam Books, N.Y., 1981.

21 Thompson, 'Defining feminism', pp. 173–4.

22 C. Bunch, 'Lesbians in revolt' in *Women and Values*, ed. M. Pearsall, Wadsworth Pub., Belmont, California, 1986, pp. 129–30 (first published in 1975).

23 G. Chester, 'I call myself a radical feminist' in *Feminist Practice: Notes from the Tenth Year*, London, In Theory Press, 1979, pp. 58–62.

24 Rowland is an Australian academic and long-standing editor of the journal, *Women's Studies International Forum*. She, like Andrea Dworkin in North America, is significant in maintaining and developing a theoretical framework for current forms of radical feminism. Her interest in new reproductive technologies provides an exemplary and contemporary conjunction of clearly articulated broad principles with the issue of control over women's bodies. R. Rowland, *Woman Herself: A Women's Studies Transdisciplinary Perspective on Self-Identity*, Oxford University Press, Melbourne, 1988; R. Rowland, *Living Laboratories: Women and the New Reproductive Technologies*, Macmillan, Sydney, 1991. See also A. Dworkin, 'Woman-hating Right and Left' in *The Sexual Liberals and the Attack on Feminism*, eds D. Leidholt and J. Raymond, Pergamon Press, N.Y., 1990.

25 However, some radical feminist writers have undertaken analysis of the economic organisation of male dominance, notably Christine Delphy. Delphy, *Close to Home*.

26 Tapper, 'Can a feminist be a liberal?'. Diverging approaches to biopolitics in radical and liberal feminism become evident in their rather different ways of dealing with bodily issues like sexual harassment, rape and abortion.

27 See, for instance, the large body of works on motherhood within

radical feminism, of which probably the most well known is A. Rich, *Of Woman Born*, W.W. Norton, N.Y., 1979.

28 A. Caddick, 'Feminism and the body', *Arena*, no. 74, 1986, p. 81.

29 A. Curthoys, 'Australian feminism since 1970' in *Australian Women: Contemporary Feminist Thought*, eds N. Grieve and A. Burns, Oxford University Press, Melbourne, 1994, p. 21.

30 A. Curthoys, 'What is the socialism in socialist feminism?', *Australian Feminist Studies*, no. 6, Autumn 1988, pp. 17–23; C. Cockburn, 'Masculinity, the Left and feminism' in *Male Order: Unwrapping Masculinity*, eds R. Chapman and J. Rutherford, Lawrence and Wishart, London, 1988, pp. 303–4..

31 Cockburn, 'Masculinity, the Left and feminism', pp. 306–7; R. Felski, 'American and British feminisms' in *Social Theory: A Guide to Central Thinkers*, ed. P. Beilharz, Allen & Unwin, Sydney, 1991, p. 22; S. Watson, 'Reclaiming social policy' in *Transitions: New Australian Feminisms*, eds B. Caine and R. Pringle, Allen & Unwin, Sydney, 1995, p. 171; H. Eisenstein, *Contemporary Feminist Thought*, Allen & Unwin, Sydney, 1984; L. Segal, *Is the Future Female?; Troubled Thoughts on Contemporary Feminism*, Virago, London, 1987.

32 Cockburn, 'Masculinity, the Left and feminism', p. 303.

33 For example, influential writers like Michele Barrett, who previously described herself as a Marxist feminist, have more recently argued that this framework largely proved unworkable. M. Barrett, *Women's Oppression Today: The Marxist/Feminist Encounter*, Verso, London, 1988, p. xxxiv.

34 In Western countries some members of communist parties, among other left-wing groupings, continue to identify themselves as Marxist feminists. In Australia, 'Resistance'—a socialist youth organisation—is one grouping where Marxist feminism is still actively espoused.

35 A. Curthoys, *For and Against Feminism: A Personal Journey into Feminist Theory and History*, Allen & Unwin, Sydney, 1988; Curthoys, 'What is the socialism in socialist feminism?'; R. Pringle, '"Socialist-Feminism" in the eighties: reply to Curthoys', *Australian Feminist Studies*, no. 6, Autumn 1988, pp. 25–30.

36 Cockburn, Eisenstein and Segal (cited in note 31) may also be mentioned here, alongside contributions in various socialist and socialist feminist journals, such as the British journal *Feminist Review*.

37 K. Bhavnani, 'Talking Racism and the editing of women's studies' in *Introducing Women's Studies: Feminist Theory and Practice*, eds

D. Richardson and V. Robinson, Macmillan, London, 1993, pp. 27–48, especially p. 45; Pringle, '"Socialist-Feminism" in the eighties: reply to Curthoys'; C. Johnson, 'Is it worth salvaging the socialism in socialist feminism?', *Australian Feminist Studies*, nos. 7/8, Summer 1988, pp. 187–91; D. Haraway, 'A manifesto for cyborgs: science, technology and socialist feminism in the 1980s', *Socialist Review*, vol. 15, no. 2, 1985, pp. 65–107; N. Fraser, 'Women, welfare and the politics of need interpretation', *Thesis Eleven*, no. 17, 1987, pp. 88–106; L. Johnson, 'Socialist feminisms' in *Feminist Knowledge: Critique and Construct*, ed. S. Gunew, Routledge, London, 1990, pp. 304–31.

38 V. Bryson, *Feminist Political Theory: An Introduction*, Macmillan, Basingstoke, Hampshire, 1992, p. 256.

39 L. Johnson, 'Socialist feminisms', ibid. pp. 304 and 312; B. Taylor, 'Lords of creation: Marxism, feminism and "utopian socialism"' in *Reader in Feminist Knowledge*, ed. S. Gunew, Routledge, 1991, pp. 360–5.

40 Karl Marx (1818–83) was a revolutionary activist and social theorist who believed that class-based societies, because inequitable are politically unstable. Class struggle, in his view, could produce necessary social change. His work was aimed at intensifying that struggle and the overthrow of inequitable class divisions in modern societies. N. Abercrombie *et al.*, *The Penguin Dictionary of Sociology*, 2nd edn, Penguin, London, 1988, pp. 146–9; D. Robertson, *The Penguin Dictionary of Politics*, 2nd edn, Penguin, London, 1993, pp. 304–6.

41 Curthoys, 'Australian feminism since 1970', pp. 20–1; L. Johnson, 'Socialist feminisms', ibid. p. 321.

42 A. Ferguson, *Blood at the Root: Motherhood, Sexuality and Male Dominance*, Pandora Press, London, 1989, pp. 20–6; R. Tong, *Feminist Thought*, 1st edn, pp. 29–53 or Tong, Feminist Thought, 2nd edn, pp. 94–114.

43 C. Beasley, *Sexual Economyths: Conceiving a Feminist Economics*, Allen & Unwin, 1994, pp. 3–27; C. Beasley, 'Charting an/other direction?: sexual economyths and suggestions for a feminist economics', *Australian Feminist Studies*, vol. 11, no. 23, 1996.

44 L. Johnson, 'Socialist feminisms', p. 310.

45 L. Vogel, *Marxism and the Oppression of Women*, Pluto Press, London, 1983; Bryson, *Feminist Political Theory*, pp. 244–7.

46 E. Grosz, 'The in(ter)vention of feminist knowledges' in *Crossing Boundaries: Feminisms and the Critique of Knowledges*, eds B. Caine *et al.*, Allen & Unwin, Sydney, 1988, pp. 92–104.

47   This form of analysis is associated with the work of Lise Vogel
     and Eli Zaretsky among others. Vogel, *Marxism and the Oppression
     of Women*; E. Zaretsky, *Capitalism, the Family and Personal Life*,
     Harper & Row, N.Y., 1976; Bryson, *Feminist Political Theory*, p.
     246; H. Hartmann, 'The Unhappy Marriage of Marxism and
     Feminism: towards a more progressive union' in *Women and
     Revolution*, ed. L. Sargent, South End Press, Boston, Ma., 1981,
     pp. 5–7.

48   Bryson, *Feminist Political Theory*, pp. 232–4; Tong, *Feminist Thought*,
     1st edn, p. 173. (Tong largely follows Jaggar's earlier account on
     this point. A. Jaggar, *Feminist Politics and Human Nature*, Rowman
     & Allanheld, Totowa, N.J., 1983.)

49   See chapter 6 of the 1st edition of Rosemarie Tong's book,
     Feminist Thought, pp. 173–93, for one interpretation of these
     different versions of socialist feminism. (The second edition is
     less clear in regard to such differentiation.)

50   J. Mitchell, *Psychoanalysis and Feminism*, Vintage Books, N.Y., 1974.

51   Jaggar, *Feminist Politics and Human Nature*; I. Young, 'Socialist
     Feminism and the limits of dual systems theory', *Socialist Review*,
     vol. 10, no. 2/3, March–June 1980, pp. 169–88.

52   Hartmann, 'The unhappy marriage of Marxism and feminism:
     towards a more progressive union', pp. 1–41.

53   M. Barrett and M. McIntosh, 'Ethnocentrism and socialist–fem-
     inist theory', *Feminist Review*, no. 20, 1985, pp. 25–47; K.
     Bhavnani and M. Coulson, 'Transforming socialist feminism: the
     challenge of racism', *Feminist Review*, no. 23, 1986, pp. 81–92.

CHAPTER 6

 1   Freudian feminists include the North American writers Nancy
     Chodorow and Dorothy Dinnerstein, as well as the English fem-
     inists Susie Orbach and Luise Eichenbaum. N. Chodorow, *The
     Reproduction of Mothering: Psychoanalysis and the Sociology of Gender*,
     University of California Press, Berkeley, 1978; D. Dinnerstein,
     *The Mermaid and the Minotaur: Sexual Arrangements and Human
     Malaise*, Harper & Row, N.Y., 1976; S. Orbach and L.
     Eichenbaum, *Understanding Women: A New Expanded Version of 'Out-
     side In . . . Inside Out'*, Penguin, Harmondsworth, 1983.

 2   Lacanian feminists include British feminists such as Juliet
     Mitchell, Jacqueline Rose and Rosalind Coward, French writers
     such as Hélène Cixous, Julia Kristeva, Luce Irigaray and more

controversially those associated with the group, 'Psychoanalyse et politique', as well as Australians like Elizabeth Grosz and Moira Gatens. For an account of the various strands of Lacanian and post-Lacanian feminism in France see C. Duchen, *Feminism in France: From May '68 to Mitterrand*, RKP, London, 1986 and C. Moses, 'Made in America: "French feminism" in United States academic discourse', *Australian Feminist Studies*, vol. 11, no. 23, April 1996, pp. 17–31; see also J. Mitchell, 'Introduction–I' in *Feminine Sexuality: Jacques Lacan and the école freudienne*, eds J. Mitchell and J. Rose, Macmillan, London, 1982, pp. 1–26; J. Rose, 'Femininity and its discontents', *Feminist Review*, no. 14, Summer 1983, pp. 5–21; R. Coward et al., 'Psychoanalysis and patriarchal structures' in *Papers on Patriarchy*, Women's Publishing Collective, Brighton, 1976, cited in L. Segal, *Is the Future Female?: Troubled Thoughts on Contemporary Feminism*, Virago, London, 1987, pp. 126–32; E. Grosz, 'Notes towards a corporeal feminism', *Australian Feminist Studies*, no. 5, Summer 1987, pp. 1–16; M. Gatens, 'A critique of the sex/gender distinction' in *Beyond Marxism: Interventions After Marx*, eds J. Allen and P. Patton, Intervention Pub., Sydney, pp. 143–60.

3 S. Freud, 'Femininity', in S. Freud, *New Introductory Lectures on Psychoanalysis*, vol. 2, Pelican, Harmondsworth, Middlesex, 1973, pp. 145–69; H. Crowley and S. Himmelweit, 'Gender and mothering' in *Knowing Women: Feminism and Knowledge*, eds H. Crowley and S. Himmelweit, Open University Press/Polity Press, Cambridge, 1992, pp. 146–51; H. Rowley and E. Grosz, 'Psychoanalysis and feminism' in *Feminist Knowledge: Critique and Construct*, ed. S. Gunew, Routledge, London and N.Y., 1990, pp. 175–92

4 Chodorow, *The Reproduction of Mothering*; N. Chodorow, 'Feminism and difference: gender, relation and difference in psychoanalytic perspective', *Socialist Review*, no. 46, 1979, pp. 51–69; see also N. Chodorow, 'The psychodynamics of the family' in *Knowing Women: Feminism and Knowledge*, eds H. Crowley and S. Himmelweit, Open University Press/Polity Press, Cambridge, 1992, pp. 153–69.

5 R. Pringle, 'Absolute sex?: unpacking the sexuality/gender relationship' in *Rethinking Sex: Social Theory and Sexuality Research*, eds R.W. Connell and G. Dowsett, Melbourne University Press, Melbourne, 1992, p. 94; C. Gilligan, *In a Different Voice: Psychological Theory and Women's Development*, Harvard University Press, Cambridge, 1983; S. Ruddick, 'Maternal thinking', *Feminist Studies*,

vol. 6, no. 2, 1980, pp. 342–67; see also C. Bacchi, *Same Difference: Feminism and Sexual Difference*, Allen & Unwin, Sydney, 1990, pp. 108–33; E. Porter, *Women and Moral Identity*, Allen & Unwin, Sydney, 1991, pp. 162–8 and 187–93.

6   L. Gordon, quoted in H. Crowley and S. Himmelweit, 'Discrimination, subordination and difference' in *Knowing Women: Feminism and Knowledge*, p. 41, see also p. 39.

7   Certain critics, for example, argue that the work of writers like Chodorow presents mothering as the singular cause of sexual oppression and inappropriately prioritises the psychological organisation of sexual identities to the exclusion of other social and cultural processes. Once again, it should be noted that such criticisms are a matter of dispute and may not be applicable to all writers in the Freudian grouping, or at least not to the same degree. See Segal, *Is the Future Female?*, pp. 143–5; I. Young, 'Is male gender identity the cause of male dominance?' in *Mothering: Essays in Feminist Theory*, ed. J. Trebilcot, Rowman and Allanheld, Totowa, N.J., 1984, pp. 138–41; C. Beasley, *Sexual Economyths: Conceiving a Feminist Economics*, Allen & Unwin, Sydney, 1994, pp. 60–1; C. MacKinnon, *Feminism Unmodified: Discourses on Life and Law*, Harvard University Press, Cambridge, 1987, pp. 38–9; C. MacKinnon, cited in R. Graycar and J. Morgan, *The Hidden Gender of Law*, The Federation Press, Sydney, 1990, pp. 47–8 and 52.

8   N. Chodorow, 'Mothering, male dominance and capitalism' in *Capitalist Patriarchy and the Case for Socialist Feminism*, ed. Z. Eisenstein, Monthly Review Press, N.Y., 1979, pp. 83–106.

9   R. Minsky, 'Lacan' in *Knowing Women: Feminism and Knowledge*, eds H. Crowley and S. Himmelweit, Open University Press/Polity Press, Cambridge, 1992, pp. 190–2; Rowley and Grosz, 'Psychoanalysis and feminism', p. 184.

10   The description of Lacanian feminist work as anti-realist enables it to be distinguished from those theoretical frameworks which, by comparison, are more inclined to allow that 'reality' can be known relatively directly and that it has a direct impact on the shape of human understanding regardless of specific cultural contexts. In broad terms Lacanian feminist thought is anti-realist in that it tends to present language and culture as shaping *how* 'reality' is experienced, whereas realists tend to perceive 'the real' as shaping culture. For an account of realist and anti-realist approaches (in the realm of legal thought), see M. Davies, *Asking the Law Question*, The Law Book Company, Sydney, 1994, pp. 120–8 and 229–40.

11 Rowley and Grosz, 'Psychoanalysis and feminism', pp. 183–6.

12 Duchen, *Feminism in France* and Moses, 'Made in America: "French feminism" in United States academic discourse'.

13 As Rowley and Grosz note, French feminists are inclined to develop 'their criticisms in terms more or less internal to [Lacan's] framework'. Rowley and Grosz, 'Psychoanalysis and feminism', p. 193.

14 Rowley and Grosz, ibid., pp. 192–3; Segal, *Is the Future Female?*, pp. 132–3; J. Lattas, 'French feminisms' in *Social Theory: A Guide to Central Thinkers*, ed. P. Beilharz, Allen & Unwin, Sydney, 1991, pp. 100–2.

15 Mitchell, 'Introduction–I', p. 23.

16 J. Rose, 'Introduction–II' in *Feminine Sexuality*, pp. 49 and 53–6.

17 Rose, 'Introduction–II', p. 56; Lattas, 'French feminisms', p. 101; J. Gallop, *Feminism and Psychoanalysis: The Daughter's Seduction*, Macmillan, London, 1982, p. 124.

18 R. Tong, *Feminist Thought: A Comprehensive Introduction*, 1st edn, Unwin Hyman, London, 1989, p. 219 or R. Tong, *Feminist Thought: A More Comprehensive Introduction*, 2nd edn, Allen & Unwin, Sydney, 1998, p. 195.

19 Lattas, 'French feminisms', p. 102.

20 J. Derrida, *Positions*, University of Chicago Press, Chicago, 1981, p. 26.

21 However this project of destabilising hierarchies must necessarily be undertaken using tools (words, language) which are already implicated in these hierarchies. Tong, *Feminist Thought*, 1st edn, p. 222 or Tong, *Feminist Thought*, 2nd edn, p. 194.

22 E. Grosz, 'Contemporary theories of power and subjectivity' in *Feminist Knowledge*, p. 101.

23 See M. Barrett and A. Phillips, 'Introduction' in *Destabilizing Theory: Contemporary Feminist Debates*, eds M. Barrett and A. Phillips, Polity, Cambridge, 1992, pp. 1–9, for one interpretation of this distinction.

24 Radical feminists are particularly notable in this regard. See Mary Daly, *Gyn/Ecology: The Meta-ethics of Radical Feminism*, Beacon Press, Boston, 1978.

25 M. Barrett, 'Words and things: materialism and method in contemporary feminist analysis' in *Destabilizing Theory*, pp. 201–6.

26 This amounts to a very thorough-going type of 'social constructivism', which might be contrasted with accounts of social life as shaped by biological (natural) determinants. See also note 10, in this chapter.

27 S. Best and D. Kellner, *Postmodern Theory: Critical Interrogations*, Guilford Press, N.Y., 1991; Barrett, 'Words and things', p. 207; Davies, *Asking the Law Question*, pp. 219–29.

28 Barrett, 'Words and things', pp. 207 and 214. On the other hand Lacanian psychoanalysis can also be viewed as containing some features aligned with postmodern/poststructuralist thought insofar as it describes the self as fragmented.

29 Lattas, 'French feminisms', p. 106.

30 See, for example, E. Grosz, 'Notes towards a corporeal feminism', *Australian Feminist Studies*, no. 5, Summer 1987, pp. 1–16; M. Gatens, 'A critique of the sex/gender distinction' in *Beyond Marxism?: Interventions after Marx*, eds J. Allen and P. Patton, Intervention Pub., Sydney, 1983, pp. 143–60; M. Gatens, *Feminism and Philosophy: Perspectives on Difference and Equality*, Polity, Oxford, 1991; R. Diprose, 'A "genethics" that makes sense' in *Cartographies: Poststructuralism and the Mapping of Bodies and Spaces*, eds R. Diprose and R. Ferrell, Allen & Unwin, Sydney, 1991, pp. 65–75; P. Rothfield, 'Bodies and subjects: medical ethics and feminism' in *Troubled Bodies: Critical Perspectives on Postmodernism, Medical Ethics and the Body*, ed. P. Komesaroff, Melbourne University Press, Melbourne, 1995, pp. 168–201.

31 Grosz argues for a corporeal feminism in which 'the body can be seen as the primary object of social production and inscription'. Grosz, 'Notes towards a Corporeal Feminism', ibid. p. 1.

32 Gatens, 'A critique of the sex/gender distinction', pp. 148–50.

33 The assertion of disembodied reason as the basis of a (sexually undifferentiated) universal human nature is particularly associated with liberalism and remains evident to a lesser extent in liberal feminism (see chapter 5).

34 M. Barrett, *Women's Oppression Today: the Marxist/Feminist Encounter*, 2nd edn, Verso, London, 1988, p. xxxi.

35 Moreover, Foucault's reservations regarding the emphasis on sexual difference in psychoanalysis (on the grounds that it rigidifies sexual categories) potentially raise doubts about why the category of sex might be prioritised above categories like race, for example.

36 E. Grosz, *Volatile Bodies: Toward a Corporeal Feminism*, Allen & Unwin, Sydney, 1994, pp. 116–17; R. Braidotti, 'The ethics of sexual difference: the case of Foucault and Irigaray', *Australian Feminist Studies*, no. 3, 1986; R. Braidotti, 'The politics of ontological difference' in *Between Psychoanalysis and Feminism*, ed. T. Brennan, Routledge, London and N.Y., 1989.

37 V. Kirby, 'Corpus delecti: the body at the scene of writing' in
    Cartographies: Poststructuralism and the Mapping of Bodies and Spaces,
    eds R. Diprose and R. Ferrell, Allen & Unwin, Sydney, 1991,
    pp. 88–100. Kirby suggests that supporters of 'French feminism'
    often interpret it as offering a textual/cultural approach to bodies
    at a distance from their actual physicality. By contrast, critics of
    'French feminist' writers are likely to accuse them of being too
    oriented towards biology and physical bodies. For one example
    of such a critic, see L. Segal, *Is the Future Female?: Troubled Thoughts
    on Contemporary Feminism*, Virago, London, 1988, pp. 132–3.

38 P. Rothfield, 'Backstage in the theatre of representation', *Arena*,
    nos. 99/100, 1992, p. 106; A. Caddick, 'Feminist and
    postmodern', *Arena*, nos. 99/100, 1992; H. Marshall, 'Our bodies
    ourselves: why we should add old fashioned empirical phenome-
    nology to the new theories of the Body', *Women's Studies
    International Forum*, vol. 19, no. 3, 1996.

39 'Corporeal' feminists appear to be developing a form of feminist
    'materialism' which resists 'realism' (see note 10 in this chapter).
    Nevertheless, those within the 'corporeal' grouping (along with
    both other adherents and critics of 'French feminism') acknow-
    ledge the dangers of discussing embodiment in concrete physical
    terms within a cultural climate where biology is taken as distinct
    from and overriding the social. See E. Probyn, 'The body which
    is not one: speaking an embodied self', *Hypatia*, vol. 6, no. 3,
    Fall 1991, pp. 111–24.

CHAPTER 7

1   Grosz has usefully summarised 'universalism', as well as 'essen-
    tialism', 'biologism' and 'naturalism', in the context of feminist
    work. E. Grosz, 'Conclusion: a note on essentialism and differ-
    ence' in *Feminist Knowledge: Critique and Construct*, ed. S. Gunew,
    Routledge, London and N.Y., 1990, pp. 334–5.

2   J. Lattas, 'French feminisms' in *Social Theory: A Guide to Central
    Thinkers*, ed. P. Beilharz, Allen & Unwin, Sydney, 1991, p. 100.

3   Writers like Gayatri Spivak, for example, draw on post-Lacanian,
    postmodern/poststructuralist and Marxist/socialist feminist
    thinking, while also dealing with imperialism and race/ethnicity.
    G. Spivak, 'French feminism in an international frame', *Yale French
    Studies*, vol. 62, 1981, pp. 154–84; G. Spivak, 'Can the subaltern
    speak?' in *Marxism and the Interpretation of Culture*, eds C. Nelson

and L. Grossberg, University of Illinios Press, Urbana, Ill.,
pp. 271–313; G. Spivak, 'The politics of translation' in *Destabilizing Theory: Contemporary Feminist Debates*, eds M. Barrett and
A. Phillips, Polity Press, Cambridge, 1992, pp. 177–200.

4   S. Bordo, 'Feminism, postmodernism and gender-scepticism' in
Feminism/Postmodernism, ed. L. Nicholson, Routledge, London,
1990, p. 149.

5   For characteristics associated with feminism, see chapter 4.

6   This contingent 'unity in diversity' or 'community' is suggested
in Lorde's comment that 'our place was the very house of
difference rather than the security of any one particular difference', as well as in notions of a 'queer community' as 'the
oxymoronic community of difference'. A. Lorde, *Zami: A New
Spelling of My Name*, Persephone Press, Watertown, Ma., 1982,
p. 226; L. Sloan, 'Beyond dialogue', *San Francisco Bay Guardian
Literary Supplement*, March 1991, p. 3; L. Duggan, 'Making it
perfectly queer', *Socialist Review*, vol. 22, no. 1, pp. 18–19.

7   In this context, I have drawn on and somewhat reworked the
approach of Ien Ang who distinguishes between two major forms
of feminist response to the consideration of differences between
women related to race/ethnicity. She outlines a 'politics of inclusion' in which diversity is simply assimilated within an already
given space designated as feminism and associates this position
with a 'unity in diversity' perspective. Ang contrasts this with a
'politics of partiality' which is predicated on the limits of 'sisterhood' and perceives feminism as a 'limited home' rather than an
all encompassing 'nation'.

    While the two approaches she outlines seem to me very
useful, in Ang's account any form of consideration of 'unity in
diversity'/community among women seems to be depicted as
equivalent to a universalising assimilationist viewpoint. It is therefore conceived as necessarily excluded from postmodern/
poststructuralist theorising around differences. I am less certain
than Ang that there is no space for a contingent sense of
unity/community which can attend to differences, and consider
that this position can be detected in some writings influenced by
postmodern/poststructuralist themes—as I have indicated in note
6 above. I. Ang, 'I'm a feminist but . . . "Other" women and
postnational feminism' in *Transitions: New Australian Feminisms*,
eds B. Caine and R. Pringle, Allen & Unwin, Sydney, 1995,
pp. 57–63.

8   C. Owens, 'The discourse of others: feminists and postmodernism'

in *The Anti-Aesthetic: Essays on Postmodern Culture*, ed. H. Foster, Bay Press, Washington, 1983, p. 57.

9   M. Davies, *Asking the Law Question*, The Law Book Company, Sydney, 1994, p. 224.

10 See, for example, different accounts of postmodernism and poststructuralism in P. Harrison, 'Narrativity and interpretation: on hermeneutical and structuralist approaches to culture', *Thesis Eleven*, no. 22, 1989, pp. 62–4; D. Tress, 'Comment on Flax's "Postmodernism and gender relations in feminist theory"', *Signs*, vol. 14, no. 1, Autumn 1988, pp. 197–8; J. Flax, 'Reply to Tress', *Signs*, vol. 14, no. 1, Autumn 1988, p. 201; P. Beilharz, *Postmodern Socialism: Romanticism, City and State*, Melbourne University Press, Melbourne, 1994, pp. 7–22; C. Weedon, *Feminist Practice and Poststructuralist Theory*, Basil Blackwell, Oxford, 1987, p. 19.

11 S. Best and D. Kellner, *Postmodern Theory: Critical Interrogations*, Guilford Press, N.Y., 1991, p. 2. This inclination to plurality—in the sense of a resistance to the singular and central place of 'man' in Western traditional social and political thought—is a first indication of some potential points of connection between postmodern and feminist thinking.

12 M. Barrett, 'Words and things' in *Destabilizing Theory: Contemporary Feminist Debates*, eds M. Barrett and A. Phillips, Polity Press, Cambridge, 1992, pp. 206–7.

13 J-F. Lyotard, *The Postmodern Condition: A Report on Knowledge*, (Theory and History of Literature, vol. 10), Manchester University Press, Manchester, 1984, pp. xxiv, 15–17, 40–1 and 81–2; F. Jameson, 'Postmodernism, or the cultural logic of late capitalism', *New Left Review*, no. 146, 1984, p. 65.

14 S. Benhabib, 'Feminism and the question of postmodernism' in *The Polity Reader in Gender Studies*, Polity Press, Cambridge, 1994, pp. 76–9; S. Hekman, 'The feminist critique of rationality' in *The Polity Reader in Gender Studies*, ibid. pp. 50–1; S. Hekman, *Gender and Knowledge: Elements of a Postmodern Feminism*, Polity Press, Cambridge, 1990, pp. 152–90.

15 However, it is worth noting at this point that the critique of foundational thought may also be applied self-reflexively to postmodern feminism since postmodernism itself can be viewed as drawing upon certain founding truth claims. Insomuch as postmodern accounts assert an improvement on 'modernist' thinking, they are unable to escape entirely the appeal to a higher truth, a procedure with which they have already taken issue. In this sense postmodern feminists cannot simply refute the

approaches pursued by other feminist traditions. Barrett, 'Words and Things', p. 210.

16 Grosz, 'Conclusion: A note on essentialism and difference', pp. 341–3; G. Spivak, 'Criticism, feminism and the institution', *Thesis Eleven*, nos. 10/11, 1984, p. 184.

17 The Enlightenment is a term describing a collection of ideas which emerged in European thought around the time of the French revolution. Enlightenment thinking is generally viewed as the ancestor of both liberalism and socialism/Marxism. D. Robertson, *The Penguin Dictionary of Politics*, 2nd edn, Penguin, London, 1993, pp. 163–4. Some feminists question the postmodern antagonism towards Enlightenment ideas concerning humanism and urge a continuing feminist engagement with such humanist ideals as equality and universal rights. P. Johnson, 'Feminism and the Enlightenment', *Radical Philosophy*, no. 63, 1993, pp. 3–12; Benhabib, 'Feminism and the question of postmodernism', pp. 88–91.

18 Postmodernism implies a suspension of belief in 'ultimate identities' and instead pays attention to instability, ambiguity and complexity in relation to the self. R. Braidotti, 'Interview', *Refractory Girl*, May 1986, pp. 9–13; J. Flax, *Psychoanalysis, Feminism and Postmodernism in the Contemporary West*, University of California Press, Berkeley, Calif., 1990, p. 32; J. Butler, *Gender Trouble: Feminism and the Subversion of Identity*, Routledge, London and N.Y., 1990, p. 143; E. Grosz, 'Contemporary theories of power and subjectivity' in *Feminist Knowledge: Critique and Construct*, ed. S. Gunew, Routledge, London and N.Y., 1990, p. 84–5.

19 Barrett, 'Words and things', p. 207.

20 M. Barrett and A. Phillips, 'Introduction' in *Destabilizing Theory: Contemporary Feminist Debates*, eds M. Barrett and A. Phillips, Polity Press, Cambridge, 1992, p. 5.

21 Lattas, 'French feminisms', p. 100.

22 Butler, *Gender Trouble*, pp. 7 and 145.

23 For example, Pringle and Watson argue that feminism cannot ground itself in an essentialist account of 'woman', gender identity or women's interests and reject notions of a common identity which unites women, but they also assert that 'along with continuing inequalities at every level, women have in common a discursive marginality'. In the light of such points, assertion of the feminine becomes a useful political tactic. R. Pringle and S. Watson, '"Women's interests"' in *Destabilizing Theory*, p. 68.

24 Spivak, 'Criticism, feminism and the institution', p. 184; K. Faith,

'Resistance: Lessons from Foucault and Feminism' in *Power/ Gender: Social Relations in Theory and Practice*, eds H. Radtke and H. Stam, Sage Pub., London, 1994, pp. 46, 53 and 57; D. Kerfoot and D. Knights, 'Into the realm of the fearful: power, identity and the gender problematic' in *Power/Gender*, p. 85.

25 Occasionally, however, poststructuralism is presented as the ecumenical label for this grouping. See, for example, Chris Weedon's usage of the term in *Feminist Practice and Poststructuralist Theory*, p. 19.

26 Derrida asserts that 'poststructuralism' was 'a word unknown in France' until it arrived from the United States as a label for certain responses to the 'structuralist problematic' within the French speaking world. J. Derrida, 'Letter to a Japanese friend' in *Derrida and Differance*, eds D. Wood and R. Bernasconi, Northwestern University Press, Evanston, 1988, p. 3.

27 While English speaking (particularly North American) feminists have directly dominated the development of the other feminist theoretical traditions mentioned so far, when employing 'French' feminist or poststructuralist approaches they have often been reliant on local interpretations/translations of distant seemingly exotic intellectual phenomena. Their analysis of these approaches may say as much about the expropriation of aspects of French speaking culture for use in disputes within English speaking feminist thought as it does about French thinking. See Curthoys on the importance of North American analyses of feminism and Moses, for discussion of North American expropriations of French culture. A. Curthoys, 'Australian Feminism since 1970' in *Australian Women: Contemporary Feminist Thought*, eds N. Grieve and A. Burns, Oxford University Press, Melbourne, 1994, pp. 16 and 18–19; C. Moses, 'Made in America: "French feminism" in United States academic discourse', *Australian Feminist Studies*, vol. 11, no. 23, April 1996, p. 27.

28 F. Saussure, *Course in General Linguistics*, Philosophical Library, N.Y., 1959, pp. 16 and 120; Barrett, 'Words and things', pp. 202–3; Pringle and S. Watson, '"Women's interests"', pp. 64–5.

29 R. Minsky, 'Lacan' in *Knowing Women: Feminism and Knowledge*, eds H. Crowley and S. Himmelweit, Open University Press/Polity Press, Cambridge, 1992, pp. 191–5; H. Rowley and E. Grosz, 'Psychoanalysis and feminism' in *Feminist Knowledge: Critique and Construct*, ed. S. Gunew, Routledge, London and N.Y., 1990, pp. 71–9.

30 Davies, *Asking the Law Question*, p. 241.

31 Barrett, 'Words and things', p. 202.

32 Hunter argues that Foucault moved even further away from a Saussurean central focus on linguistic notations (language, discourses) to the point of displacing this centrality as he began to discuss what he called dispositifs or apparatuses. Hunter asserts that Foucault's approach introduces a challenge to the residues of foundational (structuralist) thought found in the usual poststructuralist assumption that the category of discourse has universal explanatory scope. On this basis Hunter recommends retaining some separation between the ways subjectivity and language are analysed, which appears, for example, to run counter to Lacan's proposals. I. Hunter, 'From discourse to dispositif: Foucault and the study of literature', *Meridian*, vol. 10, no. 2, 1991, pp. 47–52.

33 Both unsympathetic and sympathetic commentators note that Foucault moves beyond a textualism that is more usually associated with poststructuralist thinkers like Derrida. A. Callinicos, 'Postmodernism, poststructuralism, post-Marxism?', *Theory, Culture and Society*, vol. 2, no. 3, 1985; Weedon, *Feminist Practice and Poststructuralist Theory*, pp. 20 and 22; M. Ryan, *Marxism and Deconstruction*, Johns Hopkins University Press, Baltimore, 1982, p. 63; E. Grosz, 'Derrida and the limits of philosophy', *Thesis Eleven*, no. 14, 1986, pp. 26 and 29.

34 A. Sheridan, *Michel Foucault: The Will to Truth*, Tavistock, London, 1980, p. 26.

35 E. Grosz, 'Contemporary theories of power and subjectivity' in *Feminist Knowledge*, pp. 82–92.

36 Grosz, 'Contemporary theories of power and subjectivity', p. 87.

37 Pringle and Watson, '"Women's interests"', p. 64.

38 M. Foucault, *Power/Knowledge*, Harvester Press, Brighton, 1980, pp. 93–102.

39 Foucault, interview with J.L. Brochier, quoted in Sheridan, *Michel Foucault*, p. 271.

40 Faith, 'Resistance', pp. 37–8 and 54.

41 H. Dreyfus and P. Rabinow, *Michel Foucault: Beyond Structuralism and Hermeneutics*, 2nd edn, University of Chicago Press, Chicago, 1982, p. 147.

42 Pringle and Watson, '"Women's interests"', p. 54.

43 Grosz, 'Contemporary theories of power and subjectivity', p. 92; E. Grosz, 'Notes towards a corporeal feminism, *Australian Feminist Studies*, no. 5, Summer 1987, p. 9. See also R. Braidotti, *Patterns*

of Dissonance, Blackwell, Oxford, 1991; L. McNay, 'The Foucauldian body and the exclusion of experience', *Hypatia*, vol. 6, no. 2,
1991; J. Flax, *Thinking Fragments: Psychoanalysis, Feminism and
Postmodernism in the Contemporary West*, University of California
Press, Berkeley, 1990; N. Hartsock, 'Foucault on power: a theory
for women?' in *Feminism/Postmodernism*, ed. L. Nicholson,
Routledge, London, 1990; V. Kirby, 'Corpus delecti: the body at
the scene of writing' in *Cartographies: Poststructuralism and the
Mapping of Bodies and Spaces*, eds R. Diprose and R. Ferrell, Allen
& Unwin, Sydney, 1991, p. 98.

44 See McHoul and Grace for one reply to this criticism A. McHoul
and W. Grace, *A Foucault Primer: Discourse, Power and the Subject*,
Melbourne University Press, Melbourne, 1993, pp. 119–25.

45 For links between radical anti-essentialist views of identity associated with postmodernism/poststructuralism and those
connected with 'French' feminism see N. Fraser, 'Introduction:
revaluing French feminism' in *Revaluing French Feminism: Critical
Essays on Difference, Agency and Culture*, eds N. Fraser and S. Bartky,
Indiana University Press, Bloomington and Indianapolis, 1992,
p. 7.

46 Pringle and Watson, '"Women's Interests"', p. 68; see also Spivak,
'Can the subaltern speak?'.

47 See, in the context of this concern, A. Phillips, *Hidden Hands:
Women and Economic Policies*, Pluto Press, London, 1983, p. 34.

48 Benhabib, 'Feminism and the question of postmodernism', p. 80.

49 L. McNay, *Foucault and Feminism: Power, Gender and the Self*, Polity
Press, 1992, p. 108.

50 Butler, *Gender Trouble*, p. 7; J. Butler, *Bodies That Matter: The
Discursive Limits of 'Sex'*, Routledge, N.Y., 1993, p. 224.

51 Benhabib, 'Feminism and the question of postmodernism', p. 80.

52 Butler, *Gender Trouble*, p. 4.

53 Butler, Sedgwick and de Lauretis are North American writers.
Their work is associated with feminist philosophy, literary theory
and film theory respectively. See also Wilton for a more socio-
logical approach from the UK. J. Butler, 'Critically Queer', *GLQ:
A Journal of Lesbian and Gay Studies*, vol. 1, no. 1, 1993;
E. Sedgwick, *Epistemology of the Closet*, University of California
Press, Berkeley, 1990; T. de Lauretis, *Technologies of Gender*, Indiana
University Press, Bloomington, 1987; T. Wilton, 'Genital
identities: an idiosyncratic foray into the gendering of sexualities'
in *Sexualizing the Social: Power and the Organization of Sexuality*, eds

L. Adkins and V. Merchant, Macmillan/British Sociological Association, London, 1996.

54 Foucault interviewed in B. Gallagher and A. Wilson, 'Foucault and the politics of identity', *The Advocate*, August 7, 1984.

55 Duggan, 'Making it perfectly queer', p. 20; Sedgwick, *Epistemology of the Closet*, p. 1; P. Palmer, 'Queer theory, homosexual teaching bodies and an infecting pedagogy' in *Pedagogy, Technology and the Body*, eds E. McWilliam and P. Taylor, Peter Lang, N.Y., 1996, pp. 79–80; T. de Lauretis, 'Queer theory: lesbian and gay sexualities—an introduction', *Differences: A Journal of Feminist Cultural Studies*, vol. 3, no. 2, Summer 1991, p. iv.

56 See M. Signorile, 'Gossip watch', *Outweek*, April 18, 1990 and related discussion in Duggan, 'Making it perfectly queer', pp. 15–17.

57 This critique by 'queer theorists' is directed against conceptions of the lesbian found for example in the work of Adrienne Rich and Monique Wittig. A. Rich, 'Compulsory heterosexuality and the lesbian continuum', *Signs*, vol. 5, no. 4, 1980; M. Wittig, *The Straight Mind and Other Essays*, Harvester Wheatsheaf, Hemel Hempstead, 1992.

58 de Lauretis, 'Queer theory', pp. 7–8.

59 See, for example, C. Moraga and G. Anzaldua eds, *This Bridge Called My Back: Writings by Radical Women of Colour*, Persephone Press, Watertown, Ma., 1981.

60 P. Califa, 'Gay men, lesbians and sex: doing it together', *The Advocate*, July 7, 1983; J. Zita, 'The male lesbian and the postmodernist body' in *Hypatia: A Journal of Feminist Philosophy—Special Issue: Lesbian Philosophy*, ed. C. Card, vol. 7, no. 4, 1992.

61 Nevertheless, even Butler's marked advocacy of instability does not presume that differences can proliferate endlessly or that identity is boundlessly elastic to the point of moving outside of or beyond the social. The notion of a situated sexuality/sexual identity (that is, one with some limits on its plasticity) is not quite discarded. Critics of Butler's position, including those who are sympathetic to her call to destabilise identity, pay comparatively greater attention to the possible limits on that instability. Butler, *Gender Trouble*, pp. 17–8.

62 See for instance C. Williams, 'Feminism and queer theory: allies or antagonists', *Australian Feminist Studies*, vol. 12, no. 26, 1997 and B. Creed, 'Queer theory and its discontents' in *Australian Women: Contemporary Feminist Thought*, eds N. Grieve and A. Burns, Oxford University Press, Oxford, 1994.

CHAPTER 8

1   As noted in chapter 2, refusal to afford the concept of sexual difference straightforward priority in feminist work concerned with race/ethnicity allows space for consideration of political alliances between men and women.

2   See for example, b. hooks, *Ain't I a Woman*, South End Press, Boston, Mass., 1981; b. hooks, *Feminist Theory: From Margin to Center*, South End Press, Boston, Mass., 1984, especially pp. 1–15; J. Huggins, 'Black women and women's liberation', *Hecate*, vol. 13, no. 1, 1987, pp. 77–82.

3   For example, the work of Chandra Mohanty and Gayatri Spivak shows the influence of postmodern/poststructuralist and post-Lacanian thinking. bell hooks, Kum-Kum Bhavnani, Jackie Huggins and Audre Lorde see links between aspects of their work and socialist feminism. C. Mohanty, 'Feminist encounters: locating the politics of experience' in *Destabilizing Theory*, pp. 74–92; Spivak, 'French feminism in an international frame' and 'The politics of translation'; b. hooks, *Feminist Theory: From Margin to Center*; Bhavnani, 'Talking racism and the editing of women's studies', pp. 27–48; Huggins, 'Black women and women's liberation' and J. Huggins *et al.*, Letter to the editors, *Women's Studies International Forum*, vol. 14, no. 5, 1991, pp. 506–7; A. Lorde, 'Age, race, class and sex: women redefining difference' in *Knowing Women: Feminism and Knowledge*, eds H. Crowley and S. Himmelweit, Open University/Polity Press, Cambridge, 1992, pp. 47–54.

4   Lorde, 'Age, race, class and sex', p. 48; hooks, *Ain't I a Woman*; V. Amos and P. Parmar, 'Challenging imperial feminism', *Feminist Review*, no. 17, Autumn 1984, p. 7.

5   S. Gunew and A. Yeatman, 'Introduction' in *Feminism and the Politics of Difference*, eds S. Gunew and A. Yeatman, Allen & Unwin, 1993, p. xv.

6   See Hall, and Anthias and Yuval-Davies for perspectives proposing the use of ethnicity as a cover-all term, and Mama and Kazi for the opposing view. S. Hall, *Critical Dialogue in Cultural Studies*, Routledge, London, 1996; F. Anthias and N. Yuval-Davis, 'Contextualising feminism: gender, ethnic and class divisions', *Feminist Review*, no. 15, 1983; A. Mama, 'Black women, the economic crisis and the British state', *Feminist Review*, no. 17, Autumn 1984; H. Kazi, 'The beginning of a debate long due: some observations

on ethnocentrism and socialist–feminist theory', *Feminist Review*, no. 22, 1986, pp. 88–9.

7   S. Gunew, *Framing Marginality: Multicultural Literary Studies*, Melbourne University Press, Melbourne, 1994, p. 2; J. Pettman, *Living in the Margins: Racism, Sexism and Feminism in Australia*, Allen & Unwin, Sydney, 1992.

8   Ang, 'I'm a feminist but . . . "Other" women and postnational feminism' in *Transitions: New Australian Feminisms*, eds B. Caine and R. Pringle, Allen & Unwin, Sydney, 1995, pp. 66, 68–69; K. Bhavnani, 'Talking racism and the editing of women's studies' in *Introducing Women's Studies: Feminist Theory and Practice*, eds D. Richardson and V. Robinson, Macmillan, London, 1993, p. 30 and note 2, p. 47.

9   C. West, 'The new cultural politics of difference' in *The Cultural Studies Reader*, ed. S. During, Routledge, London and N.Y., 1993, p. 210; see also A. Yeatman, 'Interlocking oppressions' in *Transitions: New Australian Feminisms*, pp. 50–1; Gunew, *Framing Marginality*, pp. 5–6; F. Rizvi, *Multiculturalism: Making Policy for a Polyethnic Society*, vol. C of *Migration, Ethnicity and Multiculturalism*, Deakin University Press, Geelong, Victoria, 1989, p. 8.

10   Mohanty, 'Feminist encounters', p. 80.

11   Ang, 'I'm a feminist but . . . "Other" women and postnational feminism', p. 66.

12   E. Spelman, *Inessential Woman: Problems of Exclusion in Feminist thought*, Beacon Press, Boston, 1988, p. 169.

13   Mohanty, 'Feminist encounters', p. 81.

14   A. Davis, *Women, Race and Class*, Women's Press, London, 1982.

15   In this context Yeatman refers to white, Western and middle class women as 'the custodians of feminism'. A. Yeatman, 'Voice and representation in the politics of difference' in *Feminism and the Politics of Difference*, p. 238.

16   Amos and Parmar, 'Challenging imperial feminism', pp. 4–6; S. Lees, 'Sex, race and culture: feminism and the limits of cultural pluralism', *Feminist Review*, no. 22, Spring 1986, p. 92; see also G. Hull *et al.* eds, *All the Women are White, All the Blacks are Men, but Some of Us are Brave*, Feminist Press, 1982; D. King, 'Multiple jeopardy, multiple consciousness: the context of a black feminist ideology', *Signs*, vol. 14, no. 1, 1988.

17   b. hooks, *Black Looks: Race and Representation*, South End Press, Boston, 1992, pp. 159–60.

18   Ang, 'I'm a feminist but . . . "Other" women and postnational feminism', p. 62.

19 M. Jolly, 'The politics of difference: feminism, colonialism and decolonisation in Vanuatu' in *Intersexions: Gender/class/culture/ethnicity*, eds G. Bottomley *et al.*, Allen & Unwin, 1991, p. 57; J. Martin, 'Multiculturalism and feminism' in *Intersexions*, ibid. pp. 125–31; see also H. Crowley and S. Himmelweit, 'Discrimination, subordination and difference: feminist perspectives' in *Knowing Women*, p. 42.

20 L. Behrendt, 'Black women and the feminist movement: implications for Aboriginal women in rights discourse', *Australian Feminist Law Journal*, vol. 1, no. 27, 1993, pp. 40–4. Huggins refers to a classic dispute over conceptions of how to speak about intraracial rape in Australia. This dispute involved, on the one hand, several Aboriginal women including Jackie Huggins and, on the other, a white anthropologist (Bell), her Aboriginal informant/co-author (Naparulla), and the avowedly radical feminist editors (Rowland/Klein) of a journal in which the joint authors (Bell/Naparulla) were published. See H. Goodall and J. Huggins, 'Aboriginal women are everywhere' in *Gender Relations in Australia: Domination and Negotiation*, eds K. Saunders and R. Evans, HBJ, Sydney, 1992, pp. 415–8; for the several views of the participants in this dispute see D. Bell (and T. Naparulla), 'Speaking about rape is everyone's business', *Women's Studies International Forum*, no. 12, 1989, pp. 403–16; Huggins *et al.*, 'Letter to the editors', *Women's Studies International Forum*, pp. 506–7; R. Klein, 'Editorial', *Women's Studies International Forum*, vol. 14, no. 5, 1991, pp. 505–6; D. Bell, 'Letter to the editors', *Women's Studies International Forum*, vol. 14, no. 5, 1991, pp. 507–13.

21 H. Carby, 'White woman listen! Black feminism and the boundaries of sisterhood' in *The Empire Strikes Back: Race and Racism in 70s Britain*, CCCS/Hutchinson, London, 1984, p. 214.

22 P. O'Shane, 'Is there any relevance in the women's movement for Aboriginal women?', *Refractory Girl*, no. 12, September 1976.

23 C. Ramazanoglu, 'Ethnocentrism and socialist–feminist theory: a response to Barrett and McIntosh', *Feminist Review*, no. 22, Spring 1986, p. 85.

24 Ramazanoglu, Ethnocentrism and socialist–feminist theory', p. 86; Ang, 'I'm a feminist but . . . "Other" women and postnational feminism', p. 63.

25 Huggins, 'Black women and women's liberation', pp. 77–8.

26 Bhavnani, 'Talking racism and the editing of women's studies', p. 34; Huggins *et al.*, 'Letter to the editors', *Women's Studies International Forum*, p. 506; b. hooks, interview in 'Let's get real

about feminism: the backlash, the myths, the movement', *Ms.*, vol. IV, no. 2, September/October 1993, pp. 38 and 42.

27 Ang, 'I'm a feminist but . . . "Other" women and postnational feminism', p. 65.

28 I am inclined for instance to locate bell hooks' approach within both trajectories as I think her earlier work could be readily designated as a form of identity politics but her recent books increasingly indicate an agenda attending to the cultural politics of difference.

29 Here I have drawn on the work of Stuart Hall and Cornel West in describing these trajectories as two interconnected 'moments' within the contemporary field of analysis attending to race/ethnicity. I have also borrowed West's terminology regarding a 'cultural politics of difference'. Hall, *Critical Dialogue in Cultural Studies*, p. 441; West, 'The new cultural politics of difference'.

30 West, 'The new cultural politics of difference', p. 210.

31 See for example B. Smith, 'Toward a black feminist criticism', in G. Hull *et al.* eds, *All the Women are White, All the Blacks are Men, but Some of Us are Brave*, Feminist Press, N.Y., 1982.

32 H. Kazi, 'The beginning of a debate long due', p. 89. Those feminists using separate terminologies to refer to race and ethnicity outline distinguishable 'black feminist' and 'multicultural feminist' perspectives. Such terms are not limited to advocates of identity politics but also surface in cultural politics of difference writings.

33 Yeatman, 'Interlocking oppressions', p. 51; King, 'Multiple jeopardy, multiple consciousness: the context of a black feminist ideology'.

34 B. Reagon, 'Coalition politics: turning the century' in *Home Girls: A Black Feminist Anthology*, ed. B. Smith, Kitchen Table/Women of Colour Press, N.Y., 1983.

35 See Ang's account of bell hooks' position on political struggle, in 'I'm a feminist but . . . "Other" women and postnational feminism', p. 68.

36 b. hooks, 'Sisterhood: political solidarity between women' in *A Reader in Feminist Knowledge*, ed. S. Gunew, Routledge, London and N.Y., 1991, pp. 29–31.

37 Hall, *Critical Dialogue in Cultural Studies*, pp. 444–6; see also hooks' determined refusal not to ignore sexism in North American black communities, any more than elsewhere, in b. hooks, *Yearning: Race, Gender and Cultural Politics*, South End Press, 1990, pp. 58–9.

38 S. Gunew, 'Feminism and the politics of irreducible differences:

multiculturalism/ethnicity/race' in *Feminism and the Politics of Difference*, p. 9.

39   Anthias and Yuval-Davis, 'Contextualising feminism: gender, ethnic and class divisions; N. Yuval-Davis, *Gender and Nation*, Sage, London, 1997.

40   See for example Langton's dynamic conception of Australian Aboriginality as a cultural construction arising out of intercultural dialogue between Aboriginal and non-Aboriginal people, rather than as a biological/cultural fixity. M. Langton, *'Well I heard it on the radio and I saw it on the television'*, Australian Film Commission, 1993.

41   G. Spivak, *In Other Worlds: Essays in Cultural Politics*, Methuen, 1987.

42   Yuval-Davis describes diaspora communities as—unlike political exiles—primarily bound up with the country in which they live, rather than their country of origin and as simultaneously belonging to and outside of both national collectivities. Yuval-Davis, *Gender and Nation*, p. 18.

43   Other related terminologies include 'postnational', 'global' and 'Third World' feminist approaches.

44   E. Said, 'Representing the colonised: anthropology's interlocutors', *Critical Inquiry*, vol. 15, no. 2, Winter 1989, p. 213.

45   Yuval-Davis, *Gender and Nation*, pp. 3–4; Ang, 'I'm a feminist but . . . "Other" women and postnational feminism', pp. 69–70.

46   Spivak, 'Criticism, feminism and the institution', *Thesis Eleven*, nos. 10/11, 1984 p. 184.

47   Ang, 'I'm a feminist but . . . "Other" women and postnational feminism', p. 67.

48   G. Joseph, 'The incompatible ménage à trois: Marxism, feminism, and racism' in *Women and Revolution: A Discussion of the Unhappy Marriage of Marxism and Feminism*, ed. L. Sargent, South End Press, Boston, Mass., 1981, pp. 91–107; Kazi, 'The beginning of a debate long due', pp. 87–91; K. Bhavnani and M. Coulson, 'Transforming socialist feminism: the challenge of racism', *Feminist Review*, no. 23, 1986, pp. 81–92; Carby, 'White woman listen!', pp. 212–35.

CONCLUSION

1   M. Ffytche,'Text appeal', *Not only Black and White*, no. 6, April 1994, p. 30.

2 'Let's get real about feminism: the backlash, the myths, the movement', *Ms.*, vol. IV, no. 2, September/October, 1993, p. 43.

Other overviews of feminist thought

DeBois, E. *et al.* Comment on Offen's article, *Signs*, vol. 15, no. 1. Autumn 1989, pp. 195–209

Delmar, R. 'What is feminism?' in *What is Feminism?*, eds J. Mitchell and A. Oakley, Basil Blackwell, Oxford, 1986, pp. 8–33

Grosz (Gross), E. 'Conclusion: what is feminist theory?' in *Feminist Challenges: Social and Political Theory*, eds C. Pateman and E. Gross, Allen & Unwin, Sydney, 1986, pp. 190–204

Gunew, S. 'Feminist knowledge: critique and construct' in *Feminist Knowledge: Critique and Construct*, ed. S. Gunew, Routledge, London, 1990, pp. 13–35

hooks, b. *et al.* 'Let's get real about feminism: the backlash, the myths, the movement', *MS.*, vol. iv, no. 2, September/October 1993, pp. 34–43

Jaggar, A. *Feminist Politics and Human Nature*, Rowman and Allanheld, Totowa, N.J., 1983, pp. 3–13

Offen, K. 'Defining feminism: a comparative historical approach', *Signs*, vol. 14, no. 1, Autumn 1988, pp. 119–57

Pateman, C. 'Introduction: the theoretical subversiveness of feminism' in *Feminist Challenges: Social and Political Theory*, eds C. Pateman and E. Gross, Allen & Unwin, Sydney, 1986, pp. 1–10

Pateman C. and Shanley, M. 'Introduction' in *Feminist Interpretations and Political Theory*, eds M. Shanley and C. Pateman, Polity Press, Cambridge, 1991, pp. 1–10

Tong, R. *Feminist Thought: A Comprehensive Introduction*, 1st edn, Unwin Hyman, London, 1989, pp. 1–9

——*Feminist Thought: A More Comprehensive Introduction*, 2nd edn, Allen & Unwin, Sydney, 1998, pp. 1–9

Bibliography

Abercrombie, N. *et al. The Penguin Dictionary of Sociology*, 2nd edn, Penguin, London, 1988

The Advertiser, Tuesday March 3, 1992, 'Appeal' section

Amos, V. and Parmar, P. 'Challenging imperial feminism', *Feminist Review*, no. 17, Autumn 1984

Ang, I. 'I'm a feminist but . . . "Other" women and postnational feminism' in *Transitions: New Australian Feminisms*, eds B. Caine and R. Pringle, Allen & Unwin, Sydney, 1995

Anthias, F. and Yuval-Davis, N. 'Contextualising feminism: gender, ethnic and class divisions, *Feminist Review*, no. 15, 1983

Aristotle, *Politics*, Book 1, trans. T. Sinclair, Penguin Books, London, 1972

Atkinson, T. *Amazon Odyssey*, Links Books, New York, 1974

Bacchi, C. *Same Difference: Feminism and Sexual Difference*, Allen & Unwin, Sydney, 1990

Barrett, M. 'Words and things: materialism and method in Contemporary feminist analysis' in *Destabilizing Theory: Contemporary Feminist Debates*, eds M. Barrett and A. Phillips, Polity Press, Cambridge, 1992

——*Women's Oppression Today: The Marxist/Feminist Encounter*, 2nd edn, Verso, London, 1988

Barrett, M. and Phillips, A. 'Introduction' in *Destabilizing Theory: Contemporary Feminist Debates*, eds M. Barrett and A. Phillips, Polity Press, Cambridge, 1992

Barrett, M. and McIntosh, M. 'Ethnocentrism and socialist–feminist theory', *Feminist Review*, no. 20, 1985

Beasley, C. 'Charting an/other direction?: sexual economyths and suggestions for a feminist economics', *Australian Feminist Studies*, vol. 11, no. 23, 1996

——*Sexual Economyths: Conceiving a Feminist Economics*, Allen & Unwin, Sydney, 1994

Behrendt, L. 'Black women and the feminist movement: implications for Aboriginal women in rights discourse', *Australian Feminist Law Journal*, vol. 1, no. 27, 1993

Beilharz, P. *Postmodern Socialism: Romanticism, City and State*, Melbourne University Press, Melbourne, 1994

Bell, D. Letter to the editors, *Women's Studies International Forum*, vol. 14, no. 5, 1991

Bell, D. and Naparulla, T. 'Speaking about rape is everyone's business', *Women's Studies International Forum*, no. 12, 1989

Benhabib, S. 'Feminism and the question of postmodernism' in *The Polity Reader in Gender Studies*, Polity Press, Cambridge, 1994

Best, S. and Kellner, D. *Postmodern Theory: Critical Interrogations*, Guilford Press, New York, 1991

Bhavnani, K. 'Talking racism and the editing of women's studies' in *Introducing Women's Studies: Feminist Theory and Practice*, eds D. Richardson and V. Robinson, Macmillan, London, 1993

Bhavnani, K. and Coulson, M. 'Transforming socialist feminism: the challenge of racism', *Feminist Review*, no. 23, 1986

Bordo, S. 'Feminism, postmodernism, and gender-scepticism' in *Feminism/Postmodernism*, ed. L. Nicholson, Routledge, London, 1990

Braidotti, R. *Patterns of Dissonance: A Study of Women in Contemporary Philosophy*, Polity Press, Cambridge, 1991

——'The politics of ontological difference' in *Between Psychoanalysis and Feminism*, ed. T. Brennan, Routledge, London and New York, 1989

——'The ethics of sexual difference: the case of Foucault and Irigaray', *Australian Feminist Studies*, no. 3, 1986

——'Interview', *Refractory Girl*, May 1986

Bryson, L. *Welfare and the State; Who Benefits?*, Macmillan, London, 1992

Bryson, V. *Feminist Political Theory: An Introduction*, Macmillan, Basingstoke, Hampshire, 1992

Bulbeck, C. 'First and Third World Feminisms', *Asian Studies Review*, vol. 15, no. 1, 1991

Butler, J. *Bodies That Matter: The Discursive Limits of 'Sex'*, Routledge, New York, 1993

——'Critically Queer', *GLQ: A Journal of Lesbian and Gay Studies*, vol. 1, no. 1, 1993

——*Gender Trouble: Feminism and the Subversion of Identity*, Routledge, London, 1990

Caddick, A. 'Feminist and postmodern', *Arena*, nos. 99/100, 1992

——'Feminism and the body', *Arena*, no. 74, 1986

Califia, P. 'Gay men, lesbians and sex: doing it together', *The Advocate*, July 7, 1983

Callinicos, A. 'Postmodernism, post-structuralism, post-Marxism?', *Theory, Culture and Society*, vol. 2, no. 3, 1985

Carby, H. 'White woman listen! Black feminism and the boundaries of sisterhood', in *The Empire Strikes Back: Race and Racism in 70s Britain*, CCCS/Hutchinson, London, 1984

Chester, G. 'I call myself a radical feminist' in *Feminist Practice: Notes from the Tenth Year*, London, In Theory Press, 1979

Chodorow, N. 'The psychodynamics of the family' in *Knowing Women: Feminism and Knowledge*, eds H. Crowley and S. Himmelweit, Open University Press/ Polity Press, Cambridge, 1992

——'Feminism and difference: gender, relation and difference in psychoanalytic perspective', *Socialist Review*, no. 46, 1979

——'Mothering, male dominance and capitalism' in *Capitalist Patriarchy and the Case for Socialist Feminism*, ed. Z. Eisenstein, Monthly Review Press, New York, 1979

——*The Reproduction of Mothering: Psychoanalysis and the Sociology of Gender*, University of California Press, Berkeley, 1978

Cixous, H. 'Sorties' in *New French Feminisms: An Anthology*, eds E. Marks and I. de Courtivron, Harvester Press, Sussex, 1981

Clark L. and Lange, L. *The Sexism of Social and Political Theory*, University of Toronto Press, Toronto, 1979

Cockburn, C. 'Masculinity, the Left and feminism' in *Male Order: Unwrapping Masculinity*, eds R. Chapman and J. Rutherford, Lawrence and Wishart, London, 1988

Creed, B. 'Queer theory and its discontents' in *Australian Women: Contemporary Feminist Thought*, eds N. Grieve and A. Burns, Oxford University Press, Oxford, 1994

Crowley, H. and Himmelweit, S. 'Discrimination, subordination and difference' in *Knowing Women: Feminism and Knowledge*, eds H. Crowley and S. Himmelweit, Open University Press/ Polity Press, Cambridge, 1992

——'Gender and mothering' in *Knowing Women: Feminism and Knowledge*, eds H. Crowley and S. Himmelweit, Open University Press/ Polity Press, Cambridge, 1992

Curthoys, A. 'Australian feminism since 1970' in *Australian Women: Contemporary Feminist Thought*, eds N. Grieve and A. Burns, Oxford University Press, Melbourne, 1994

——'What is the socialism in socialist feminism?', *Australian Feminist Studies*, no. 6, Autumn 1988

——*For and Against Feminism: A Personal Journey into Feminist Theory and History*, Allen & Unwin, Sydney, 1988

Daly, M. *Gyn/Ecology: The Meta-ethics of Radical Feminism*, Beacon Press, Boston, 1978

Davies, M. *Asking the Law Question*, The Law Book Company, Sydney, 1994

Davis, A. *Women, Race and Class*, Women's Press, London, 1982

de Beauvoir, S. *The Second Sex*, trans. and ed. H. Parshley, Vintage Books, New York, 1974

de Lauretis, T. 'Queer theory: lesbian and gay sexualities—an introduction', *Differences: A Journal of Feminist Cultural Studies*, vol. 3, no. 2, Summer 1991

——*Technologies of Gender*, Indiana University Press, Bloomington, 1987

Delmar, R. 'What is feminism?' in *What is Feminism?*, eds J. Mitchell and A. Oakley, Basil Blackwell, Oxford, 1986

Delphy, C. 'The main enemy' in C. Delphy, *Close to Home: A Materialist Analysis of Women's Oppression*, trans. and ed. D. Leonard, Hutchinson, London, 1984

Derrida, J. 'Letter to a Japanese friend' in *Derrida and Différance*, eds D. Wood and R. Bernasconi, Northwestern University Press, Evanston, 1988

——*Positions*, University of Chicago Press, Chicago, 1981

Dinnerstein, D. *The Mermaid and the Minotaur: Sexual Arrangements and Human Malaise*, Harper & Row, New York, 1976

Diprose, R. 'A "genethics" that makes sense' in *Cartographies: Poststructuralism and the Mapping of Bodies and Spaces*, eds R. Diprose and R. Ferrell, Allen & Unwin, Sydney, 1991

Donovan, J. *Feminist Theory*, Unger, New York, 1985

Dreyfus, H. and Rabinow, P. *Michel Foucault: Beyond Structuralism and Hermeneutics*, 2nd edn, University of Chicago Press, Chicago, 1982

Duchen, C. *Feminism in France: From May '68 to Mitterrand*, RKP, London, 1986

Duggan, L. 'Making it perfectly queer', *Socialist Review*, vol. 22, no. 1

Dworkin, A. 'Woman-hating Right and Left' in *The Sexual Liberals and the Attack on Feminism*, eds D. Leidholt and J. Raymond, Pergamon Press, New York, 1990

Eisenstein, H. *Gender Shock: Practising Feminism on Two Continents*, Allen & Unwin, Sydney, 1991

——*Contemporary Feminist Thought*, Allen & Unwin, Sydney, 1984

Eisenstein, Z. *The Radical Future of Liberal Feminism*, North Eastern University Press, Boston, 1986

Elshtain, J. *Public Man, Private Woman*, Princeton University Press, Princeton, 1981

Faith, K. 'Resistance: lessons from Foucault and feminism', in

Power/Gender: Social Relations in Theory and Practice, eds H. Radtke and H. Stam, Sage, London, 1994

Faust, B. 'Australian-style feminism: what a gift to the world', *The Australian*, 22 February 1994

Felski, R. 'American and British feminisms' in *Social Theory: A Guide to Central Thinkers*, ed. P. Beilharz, Allen & Unwin, Sydney, 1991

Ferguson, A. *Blood at the Root: Motherhood, Sexuality and Male Dominance*, Pandora Press, London, 1989

Firestone, S. *The Dialectic of Sex: The Case for Feminist Revolution*, Bantam Books, New York, 1981

Flax, J. *Psychoanalysis, Feminism and Postmodernism in the Contemporary West*, University of California Press, Berkeley, Calif., 1990

——*Thinking Fragments: Psychoanalysis, Feminism and Postmodernism in the Contemporary West*, University of California Press, Berkeley, 1990

——'Reply to Tress', *Signs*, vol. 14, no. 1, Autumn 1988

Foucault, M. *Power/Knowledge*, Harvester Press, Brighton, 1980

Fraser, N. 'Introduction: revaluing French feminism' in *Revaluing French Feminism: Critical Essays on Difference, Agency and Culture*, eds N. Fraser and S. Bartky, Indiana University Press, Bloomington and Indianapolis, 1992

——'Women, welfare and the politics of need interpretation', *Thesis Eleven*, no. 17, 1987

Freud, S. 'Femininity', in S. Freud, *New Introductory Lectures on Psychoanalysis*, vol. 2, Pelican, Harmondsworth, Middlesex, 1973

Gallagher, B. and Wilson, A. 'Foucault and the politics of identity', *The Advocate*, August 7, 1984

Gallop, J. *Reading Lacan*, Cornell University Press, Ithaca, 1985

——*Feminism and Psychoanalysis: The Daughter's Seduction*, Macmillan, London, 1982

Gatens, M. 'The dangers of a woman-centred philosophy' in *The Polity Reader in Gender Studies*, Polity Press, Cambridge, 1994

——'Power, bodies and difference' in *Destabilizing Theory: Contemporary Feminist Debates*, eds M. Barrett and A. Phillips, Polity, Cambridge, 1992

——*Feminism and Philosophy: Perspectives on Difference and Equality*, Polity, Oxford, 1991

——'Feminism, philosophy and riddles without answers', in *Feminist Challenges: Social and Political Theory*, eds. C. Pateman and E. Gross, Allen & Unwin, Sydney, 1986

——'A critique of the sex/gender distinction' in *Beyond Marxism: Interventions After Marx*, eds J. Allen and P. Patton, Intervention, Sydney, 1983

George, V. and Wilding, P. *Ideology and Social Welfare*, RKP, London, 1976

Gilligan, C. *In a Different Voice: Psychological Theory and Women's Development*, Harvard University Press, Cambridge, 1983

Goodall, H. and Huggins, J. 'Aboriginal women are everywhere' in *Gender Relations in Australia: Domination and Negotiation*, eds K. Saunders and R. Evans, HBJ, Sydney, 1992

Grant, J. *Fundamental Feminism: Contesting the Core Concepts of Feminist Theory*, Routledge, London, 1993

Graycar, R. and Morgan, J. *The Hidden Gender of Law*, The Federation Press, Sydney, 1990

Grimshaw, J. *Feminist Philosophers: Women's Perspectives on Philosophical Traditions*, Wheatsheaf Books, Brighton, 1986

Grosz (Gross), E. *Volatile Bodies: Toward a Corporeal Feminism*, Allen & Unwin, Sydney, 1994

——'Contemporary theories of power and subjectivity' in *Feminist Knowledge: Critique and Construct*, ed. S. Gunew, Routledge, London and New York, 1990

——'Conclusion: a note on essentialism and difference' in *Feminist Knowledge: Critique and Construct*, ed. S. Gunew, Routledge, London and New York, 1990

——'The in(ter)vention of feminist knowledges' in *Crossing Boundaries: Feminisms and the Critique of Knowledges*, eds B. Caine et al., Allen & Unwin, Sydney, 1988

——'Notes towards a corporeal feminism', *Australian Feminist Studies*, no. 5, Summer, 1987

——'Conclusion: what is feminist theory?' in *Feminist Challenges: Social and Political Theory*, eds C. Pateman and E. Gross, Allen & Unwin, Sydney, 1986

——'Derrida and the limits of philosophy', *Thesis Eleven*, no. 14, 1986

Gunew, S. *Framing Marginality: Multicultural Literary Studies*, Melbourne University Press, Melbourne, 1994

——'Feminism and the politics of irreducible differences: multiculturalism/ethnicity/race' in *Feminism and the Politics of Difference*, eds S. Gunew and A. Yeatman, Allen & Unwin, Sydney, 1993

Gunew, S. and Yeatman, A. 'Introduction' in *Feminism and the Politics of Difference*, eds S. Gunew and A. Yeatman, Allen & Unwin, Sydney, 1993

Hall, S. *Critical Dialogue in Cultural Studies*, Routledge, London, 1996

Haraway, D. 'A manifesto for cyborgs: science, technology and socialist feminism in the 1980s', *Socialist Review*, vol. 15, no. 2, 1985

Harrison, P. 'Narrativity and interpretation: on hermeneutical and structuralist approaches to culture', *Thesis Eleven*, no. 22, 1989

Hartmann, H. 'The unhappy marriage of Marxism and feminism: towards a more progressive union' in *Women and Revolution: A Discussion of the Unhappy Marriage of Marxism and Feminism*, ed. L. Sargent, South End Press, Boston, Mass., 1981

Hartsock, N. 'Foucault on power: a theory for women?', in *Feminism/Postmodernism*, ed. L. Nicholson, Routledge, London, 1990

Hekman, S. 'The feminist critique of rationality' in *The Polity Reader in Gender Studies*, Polity Press, Cambridge, 1994

——*Gender and Knowledge: Elements of a Postmodern Feminism*, Polity Press, Cambridge, 1990

hooks, b. Interview in 'Let's get real about feminism: the backlash, the myths, the movement', *Ms.*, vol. IV, no. 2, 1993

——*Black Looks: Race and Representation*, South End Press, Boston, 1992

——'Sisterhood: political solidarity between women' in *A Reader in Feminist Knowledge*, ed. S. Gunew, Routledge, London and New York, 1991

——*Yearning: Race, Gender and Cultural Politics*, South End Press, Boston, Mass., 1990

——*Feminist Theory: From Margin to Center*, South End Press, Boston, Mass., 1984

——*Ain't I a Woman*, South End Press, Boston, Mass., 1981

Huggins, J. 'A contemporary view of Aboriginal women's relationship to the white women's movement' in *Australian Women: Contemporary Feminist Thought*, eds N. Grieve and A. Burns, Oxford University Press, Melbourne, 1994

——'Black women and women's liberation', *Hecate*, vol. 13, no. 1, 1987

Huggins, J. et al. 'Letter to the editors', *Women's Studies International Forum*, vol. 14, no. 5, 1991

Hull, G. et al. eds *All the Women are White, All the Blacks are Men, but Some of Us are Brave*, Feminist Press, 1982

Hunter, I. 'From discourse to dispositif: Foucault and the study of literature', *Meridian*, vol. 10, no. 2, 1996

Jaggar, A., *Feminist Politics and Human Nature*, Rowman & Allanheld, Totowa, N.J., 1983

Jameson, F. 'Postmodernism, or the cultural logic of late capitalism', *New Left Review*, no. 146, 1984

Jardine, A. *Gynesis: Configurations of Woman and Modernity*, Cornell University Press, Ithaca/London, 1985

Johnson, C. 'Is it worth salvaging the socialism in socialist feminism?', *Australian Feminist Studies*, nos. 7/8, Summer 1988

Johnson, L. 'Socialist feminisms' in *Feminist Knowledge: Critique and Construct*, ed. S. Gunew, Routledge, London and New York, 1990

Johnson, P. 'Feminism and the Enlightenment', *Radical Philosophy*, no. 63, 1993

Jolly, M. 'The politics of difference: feminism, colonialism and decolonisation in Vanuatu' in *Intersexions: Gender/Class/Culture/Ethnicity*, eds G. Bottomley *et al.*, Allen & Unwin, Sydney, 1991

Joseph, G. 'The incompatible ménage à trois: Marxism, feminism, and racism' in *Women and Revolution: A Discussion of the Unhappy Marriage of Marxism and Feminism*, ed. L. Sargent, South End Press, Boston, Mass., 1981

Kazi, H. 'The beginning of a debate long due: some observations on ethnocentrism and socialist–feminist theory', *Feminist Review*, no. 22, 1986

Kerfoot D. and Knights, D. 'Into the realm of the fearful: power, identity and the gender problematic' in *Power/Gender: Social Relations in Theory and Practice*, eds H. Radtke and H. Stam, Sage, London, 1994

King, D. 'Multiple jeopardy, multiple consciousness: the context of a black feminist ideology', *Signs*, vol. 14, no. 1, 1988.

Kirby, V. 'Corpus delecti: The body at the scene of writing' in *Cartographies: Poststructuralism and the Mapping of Bodies and Spaces*, eds R. Diprose and R. Ferrell, Allen & Unwin, Sydney, 1991

Klein, R. Editorial, *Women's Studies International Forum*, vol. 14, no. 5, 1991

Langton, M. '*Well I heard it on the radio and I saw it on the television*', Australian Film Commission, 1993

Lattas, J. 'French feminisms' in *Social Theory: A Guide to Central Thinkers*, ed. P. Beilharz, Allen & Unwin, Sydney, 1991

Lees, S. 'Sex, race and culture: feminism and the limits of cultural pluralism', *Feminist Review*, no. 22, Spring 1986

Lorde, A. 'Age, race, class and sex: women redefining difference' in *Knowing Women: Feminism and Knowledge*, eds H. Crowley and S. Himmelweit, Open University Press/ Polity Press, Cambridge, 1992

——Zami: *A New Spelling of My Name*, Persephone Press, Watertown, Mass., 1982

Lyotard, J-F. *The Postmodern Condition: A Report on Knowledge* (Theory and History of Literature, vol. 10), Manchester University Press, Manchester, 1984

MacKinnon, C. *Feminism Unmodified: Discourses on Life and Law*, Harvard University Press, Cambridge, 1987

Mama, A. 'Black women, the economic crisis and the British state', *Feminist Review*, no. 17, Autumn 1984

March, A. 'Female invisibility in androcentric sociological theory', *Insurgent Sociologist*, vol. 11, no. 2

BIBLIOGRAPHY

Marshall, H. 'Our bodies ourselves: why we should add some old fashioned empirical phenomenology to the new theories of the body', *Women's Studies International Forum*, vol. 19, no. 3, 1996

Martin, J. 'Multiculturalism and feminism' in *Intersexions: Gender/Class/Culture/Ethnicity*, eds G. Bottomley *et al.*, Allen & Unwin, Sydney, 1991

McHoul, A. and Grace, W. *A Foucault Primer: Discourse, Power and the Subject*, Melbourne University Press, Melbourne, 1993

Millett, K. *Sexual Politics*, Avon Books, New York, 1971

McNay, L. *Foucault and Feminism: Power, Gender and the Self*, Polity Press, Cambridge, 1992

——'The Foucauldian body and the exclusion of experience', *Hypatia*, vol. 6, no. 2, 1991

Minsky, R. 'Lacan' in *Knowing Women: Feminism and Knowledge*, eds H. Crowley and S. Himmelweit, Open University Press/Polity Press, Cambridge, 1992

Mitchell, J. 'Introduction—I' in *Feminine Sexuality: Jacques Lacan and the école freudienne*, eds J. Mitchell and J. Rose, Macmillan, London, 1982

——*Psychoanalysis and Feminism*, Vintage Books, New York, 1974

Mohanty, C. 'Feminist encounters: locating the politics of experience' in *Destabilizing Theory: Contemporary Feminist Debates*, eds M. Barrett and A. Phillips, Polity, Cambridge, 1992

Moller-Okin, S. 'Rousseau's natural woman', *Journal of Politics*, no. 41, 1979

Moraga, C. and Anzaldua, G. eds *This Bridge Called My Back: Writings by Radical Women of Colour*, Persephone Press, Watertown, Mass., 1981

Morgan, R. *Sisterhood is Global*, Anchor Press/Doubleday, New York, 1984

——*Going Too Far*, Vintage Books, New York, 1978

Moses, C. 'Made in America: "French feminism" in United States academic discourse', *Australian Feminist Studies*, vol. 11, no. 23, April, 1996

O'Brien, M. *The Politics of Reproduction*, RKP, London, 1981

Offen, K. 'Defining feminism: a comparative historical approach', *Signs*, vol. 14, no. 1, 1988

Orbach, S. and Eichenbaum, L. *Understanding Women: A New Expanded Version of 'Outside In . . . Inside Out'*, Penguin, Harmondsworth, 1983

O'Shane, P. 'Is there any relevance in the women's movement for Aboriginal women?', *Refractory Girl*, no. 12, September 1976

Owens, C. 'The discourse of others: feminists and postmodernism' in *The Anti-Aesthetic: Essays on Postmodern Culture*, ed. H. Foster, Bay Press, Washington, 1983

Palmer, P. 'Queer theory, homosexual teaching bodies, and an infecting pedagogy', in *Pedagogy, Technology, and the Body*, eds E. McWilliam and P. Taylor, Peter Lang, New York, 1996

Pateman, C. *The Sexual Contract*, Polity, Oxford, 1988

——'Introduction: the theoretical subversiveness of feminism' in *Feminist Challenges: Social and Political Theory*, eds C. Pateman and E. Gross, Allen & Unwin, Sydney, 1986

Pateman C. and Shanley, M. 'Introduction' in *Feminist Interpretations and Political Theory*, eds M. Shanley and C. Pateman, Polity Press, Cambridge, 1991

Pettman, J. *Living in the Margins: Racism, Sexism and Feminism in Australia*, Allen & Unwin, Sydney, 1992

Phillips, A. *Hidden Hands: Women and Economic Policies*, Pluto Press, London, 1983

Porter, E. *Women and Moral Identity*, Allen & Unwin, Sydney, 1991

Pringle, R. 'Absolute sex?: unpacking the sexuality/gender relationship' in *Rethinking Sex: Social Theory and Sexuality Research*, eds R. W. Connell and G. Dowsett, Melbourne University Press, Melbourne, 1992

——'"Socialist–Feminism" in the eighties: reply to Curthoys', *Australian Feminist Studies*, no. 6, Autumn 1988

Pringle, R. and Watson, S. '"Women's interests" and the post–structuralist state' in *Destabilizing Theory: Contemporary Feminist Debates*, eds M. Barrett and A. Phillips, Polity Press, Cambridge, 1992

Probyn, E. 'The Body which is not one: speaking an embodied self', *Hypatia*, vol. 6, no. 3, Fall 1991

Ramazanoglu, C. 'Ethnocentrism and socialist–feminist theory: a response to Barrett and McIntosh', *Feminist Review*, no. 22, Spring 1986

Reagon, B. 'Coalition politics: turning the century' in *Home Girls: A Black Feminist Anthology*, ed. B. Smith, Kitchen Table/Women of Colour Press, New York, 1983

Rich, A. 'Compulsory heterosexuality and lesbian existence', *Signs*, vol. 5, no. 4, Summer 1980

——*Of Woman Born*, W.W. Norton, New York, 1979

Richards, J. *The Sceptical Feminist: A Philosophical Enquiry*, Penguin, Harmondsworth, 1982

Riley, D. *Am I that Name?: Feminism and the Category of 'Women' in History*, Macmillan, Basingstoke, 1988

Rizvi, F. *Multiculturalism: Making Policy for a Polyethnic Society*, vol. C of *Migration, Ethnicity and Multiculturalism*, Deakin University Press, Geelong, Victoria, 1989

Robertson, D. *The Penguin Dictionary of Politics*, 2nd edn, Penguin, London, 1993

Rose, J. 'Femininity and its Discontents', *Feminist Review*, no. 14, Summer, 1983

——'Introduction—II' in *Feminine Sexuality: Jacques Lacan and the école freudienne*, eds J. Mitchell and J. Rose, Macmillan, London, 1982

Rothfield, P. 'Bodies and subjects: medical ethics and feminism' in *Troubled Bodies: Critical Perspectives on Postmodernism, Medical Ethics and the Body*, ed. P. Komesaroff, Melbourne University Press, Melbourne, 1995

——'Backstage in the theatre of representation', *Arena*, nos. 99/100, 1992

——'New wave feminism: feminism and postmodernism' in *Discourse and Difference: Post-structuralism, Feminism and the Moment of History*, eds A. Milner and C. Worth, Centre for General and Comparative Literature (Monash University), Clayton, Victoria, 1990

Rowland, R. *Living Laboratories: Women and the New Reproductive Technologies*, Macmillan, Sydney, 1991

——*Woman Herself: A Women's Studies Transdisciplinary Perspective on Self-Identity*, Oxford University Press, Melbourne, 1988

Rowland, R. and Klein, R. 'Radical feminism: critique and construct' in *Feminist Knowledge: Critique and Construct*, ed. S. Gunew, Routledge, London and New York, 1990

Rowley, H. and Grosz, E. 'Psychoanalysis and feminism', in *Feminist Knowledge: Critique and Construct*, ed. S. Gunew, Routledge, London and New York, 1990

Ruddick, S. 'Maternal thinking', *Feminist Studies*, vol. 6, no. 2, 1980,

Ryan, M. *Marxism and Deconstruction*, Johns Hopkins University Press, Baltimore, 1982

Said, E. 'Representing the colonised: anthropology's interlocutors', *Critical Inquiry*, vol. 15, no. 2, Winter 1989

Saussure, F. *Course in General Linguistics*, Philosophical Library, New York, 1959

Sawer, M. 'Feminism and the state; Australia compared', seminar paper delivered to the Department of Politics, University of Adelaide, 1992

——'Why has the women's movement had more influence on government in Australia than elsewhere?' in *Australia Compared: People, Policies and Politics*, ed. F. Castles, Allen & Unwin, Sydney, 1991

Saxonhouse, A. 'On Aristotle' in *Feminist Interpretations and Political Theory*, eds M. Shanley and C. Pateman, Polity Press, Cambridge, 1991

Scott, J. 'Deconstructing equality–versus–difference: or, the uses of poststructuralist theory for feminism', *Feminist Studies*, vol. 14, no. 33, 1988

Sedgwick, E. *Epistemology of the Closet*, University of California Press, Berkeley, 1990

Segal, L. *Is the Future Female?: Troubled thoughts on Contemporary Feminism*, Virago, London, 1988

Sheridan, A. *Michel Foucault: The Will to Truth*, Tavistock, London, 1980

Signorile, M. 'Gossip watch', *Outweek*, 18 April 1990

Sloan, L. 'Beyond dialogue', *San Francisco Bay Guardian Literary Supplement*, March 1991

Smith, B. 'Toward a black feminist criticism' in G. Hull *et al.* eds *All the Women are White, All the Blacks are Men, but Some of Us are Brave*, Feminist Press, New York, 1982

Spelman, E. 'On de Beauvoir' in *Feminist Interpretations and Political Theory*, eds M. Shanley and C. Pateman, Polity Press, Cambridge, 1991

——*Inessential Woman: Problems of Exclusion in Feminist Thought*, Beacon Press, Boston, 1988

Spivak, G. 'The politics of translation' in *Destabilizing Theory: Contemporary Feminist Debates*, eds M. Barrett and A. Phillips, Polity Press, Cambridge, 1992

——'Can the subaltern speak?' in *Marxism and the Interpretation of Culture*, eds C. Nelson and L. Grossberg, University of Illinois Press, Urbana, Ill., 1988

——*In Other Worlds: Essays in Cultural Politics*, Methuen, New York, 1987

——'Criticism, feminism and the institution', *Thesis Eleven*, nos. 10/11, 1984

——'French feminism in an international frame', *Yale French Studies*, vol. 62, 1981

Stacey, J. 'Untangling feminist theory' in *Introducing Women's Studies: Feminist Theory and Practice*, eds D. Richardson and V. Robinson, Macmillan, London, 1993

Stretton, H. and Orchard, L. *Public Goods, Public Enterprise, Public Choice: Theoretical Foundations of the Contemporary Attack on Government*, Macmillan/St Martin's Press, London/New York, 1994

Summers, A. 'Feminism on two continents: The women's movement in Australia and the United States' in *Australian Women: Contemporary Feminist Thought*, eds N. Grieve and A. Burns, Oxford University Press, Melbourne, 1994

Tapper, M. 'Can a feminist be a liberal?', *Australasian Journal of Philosophy*, no. 64, Supplement, June, 1986,

Taylor, B. 'Lords of creation: Marxism, feminism and "utopian socialism"' in *Reader in Feminist Knowledge*, ed. S. Gunew, Routledge, New York, 1991

Theile, B. 'Vanishing acts in social and political thought: tricks of the trade' in *Feminist Challenges: Social and Political Theory*, eds C. Pateman and E. Gross, Allen & Unwin, Sydney, 1986

Thompson, D. 'Defining feminism', *Australian Feminist Studies*, no. 20, Summer 1994

Tong, R. *Feminist Thought: A Comprehensive Introduction*, 1st edn, Unwin Hyman, London, 1989

——*Feminist thought: A More Comprehensive Introduction*, 2nd edn, Allen & Unwin, Sydney, 1998

Tress, D. 'Comment on Flax's "Postmodernism and Gender Relations in Feminist Theory"', *Signs*, vol. 14, no. 1, Autumn 1988

Tuttle, L. *Encyclopedia of Feminism*, Arrow Books, London, 1987

Vogel, L. *Marxism and the Oppression of Women*, Pluto Press, London, 1983

Watson, S. 'Reclaiming social policy' in *Transitions: New Australian Feminisms*, eds B. Caine and R. Pringle, Allen & Unwin, Sydney, 1995

Weedon, C. *Feminist Practice and Poststructuralist Theory*, Basil Blackwell, Oxford, 1987

Wendell, S. 'A (Qualified) defense of liberal feminism', *Hypatia*, vol. 2, no. 2, Summer 1987

West, C. 'The new cultural politics of difference' in *The Cultural Studies Reader*, ed. S. During, Routledge, London and New York, 1993

Williams, C. 'Feminism and queer theory: allies or antagonists', *Australian Feminist Studies*, vol. 12, no. 26, 1997

Wilton, T. 'Genital identities: an idiosyncratic foray into the gendering of sexualities' in *Sexualizing the Social: Power and the Organization of Sexuality*, eds L. Adkins and V. Merchant, Macmillan/British Sociological Association, London, 1996

Wittig, M. *The Straight Mind and Other Essays*, Harvester Wheatsheaf, Hemel Hempstead, 1992

Wolf, N. *Fire with Fire: The New Female Power and How It Will Change the 21st Century*, Chatto and Windus, London, 1993

——'How to be a feminist and still love men', *Cleo*, February, 1993

——Interview in 'Let's get real about feminism, the backlash, the myths, the movement', *Ms.*, vol. IV, no. 2, 1993

Wolf, N. *The Beauty Myth*, Chatto & Windus, London, 1990

Yeatman, A. 'Interlocking oppressions' in *Transitions: New Australian Feminisms*, eds B. Caine and R. Pringle, Allen & Unwin, Sydney, 1995

——'Voice and representation in the politics of difference' in *Feminism and the Politics of Difference*, eds S. Gunew and A. Yeatman, Allen & Unwin, 1993

Young, I. 'Humanism, Gynocentrism and feminist politics', *Women's Studies International Forum*, vol. 8, no. 3, 1985

——'Is male gender identity the cause of male dominance?', in *Mothering: Essays in Feminist Theory*, ed. J. Trebilcot, Rowman & Allanheld, Totowa, N.J., 1984

——'Socialist feminism and the limits of dual systems theory', *Socialist Review*, vol. 10, no. 2/3, March–June, 1980

Yuval-Davis, N. *Gender and Nation*, Sage, London, 1997

Zaretsky, E. *Capitalism, the Family and Personal Life*, Harper & Row, New York, 1976

Zita, J. 'The male lesbian and the postmodernist body' in *Hypatia: A Journal of Feminist Philosophy—Special Issue: Lesbian Philosophy*, ed. C. Card, vol. 7, no. 4, 1992

Index

INDEX

CPSIA information can be obtained
at www.ICGtesting.com
Printed in the USA
FOW03n1723260917
0387FF